90 DAYS

Daily Reflections for Lent and Easter

Kay Murdy

Resource Publications, Inc.
San Jose, California

Editorial director: Kenneth Guentert
Managing editor: Elizabeth J. Asborno
Editorial assistant: Mary Ezzell

Reprint Department
Resource Publications, Inc.
160 E. Virginia Street #290
San Jose, CA 95112-5876

Library of Congress Cataloging in Publication Data
Murdy, Kay, 1936-
    90 days : daily reflections for Lent and Easter / Kay Murdy.
        p.   cm.
    Includes index.
    ISBN 0-89390-306-X
    1. Lent—Prayer-books and devotions—English. 2. Holy
Week—Prayer-books and devotions—English. 3. Easter—
Prayer-books and devotions—English. 4. Eastertide—
Prayer-books and devotions—English. 5. Ascension Day—
Prayer-books and devotions—English. 6. Ascensiontide—
Prayer-books and devotions—English. 7. Pentecost
Festival—Prayer-books and devotions—English. 8. Catholic
Church—Prayer-books and devotions—English. I. Title.
II. Title: Ninety days.
BX2170.L4M87 1994
242'.34—dc20   94-33529

Printed in the United States of America

99 98 97 96 95 | 5 4 3 2 1

To my husband, Bob,
for his faithful support,
to my family and friends
for their encouragement,
and to my mother,
my beautiful Rose,
who in her dying
is living the paschal mystery of our Lord

Contents

Part Two: Easter Sunday to Pentecost Sunday

Acknowledgments

Introduction

The modern world tends to compartmentalize life—it's either work or play, secular or holy. The biblical world sees life as a meaningful whole. In the church's division of the year into times and seasons, we sometimes get the impression that our faith life is divided too. The early church celebrated Easter for many years before it celebrated Lent. Gradually the church came to the realization that the cross and the crown recall the same mystery, and cannot be separated. The Easter Triduum reflects this unity. It is celebrated as one long day instead of three individual days. Even three days are not enough to celebrate the Paschal Mystery. The Paschal Mystery means God's plan to effect our redemption through Christ's saving death, resurrection, ascension and sending of the Spirit. Christians participate in this mystery throughout their lives. Baptism is a sign that we have died to our former lives and have risen to a new life in Christ, not once, but every day. In the Eucharist, we remember the Lord's giving his body for us and pouring out his blood for us. We enter into this sacred mystery through our "Amen," our daily "Yes!" that expresses our willingness to offer ourselves to God and others.

During the Forty Days of Lent we examine ourselves as do those who are preparing for baptism. We ask ourselves: "What are we doing to reform our lives so as to be the people of God? How can we announce Jesus' message that God's kingdom is at hand?"

During the Fifty Days of Easter we ask ourselves: "How can we announce the good news of Christ's saving work? How can we live our lives in praise and thanksgiving to God?"

On Pentecost we ask: "What vision of God's kingdom is the Spirit giving us? How can we put it in action?"

The Spirit says: "Go and do it!" Pentecost is not the last act in a drama. Our lives in Christ are a continuous unfolding mystery.

These ninety days—forty plus fifty—are just a microcosm of eternity.

Part One

Ash Wednesday to Holy Saturday

Ash Wednesday

Mt 6:1–6,16–18
 Joel 2:12–18; Ps 51; 2 Cor 5:20–6:2

Your Father who sees in secret will reward you.
— Mt 6:18

To Note

Ashes are an ancient symbol of penance. In the early
church, public penitents put on sackcloth and ashes
to show their remorse for sin. Today, ashes from last
year's palm branches are used in the liturgy to remind us that human life with all its glamour is soon
ended. The signing with ashes on the foreheads of
the faithful is a solemn call to penance: "Remember!
You are dust and to dust you shall return." It is also
a reminder of the joy of eternal life: "Repent, and
believe the good news!"

To Understand

"Blow the trumpet! Proclaim a fast! Call an assembly! Gather the people! Notify the congregation!"
The prophet Joel is relentless in his announcement
that the day of the Lord is near. Paul is equally
emphatic: "In Christ's name, be reconciled to God!"
When talking about the need for repentance, Jesus
seems to contradict Joel. He says, "Don't blow a
horn!" What Jesus is telling us is, "Don't blow your
own horn." Jesus teaches us to examine our motives

2

when performing the pious acts of almsgiving, prayer, and fasting. Giving alms should be a gesture of compassion toward the poor, not a way to display my generosity. Prayer should express my love of God; it is not a means to win approval. Fasting should express my sorrow for sin. It has no value if done to let others know how holy I am. No matter how good the works, if my primary motive is to enhance my own image, I already have my reward in the way I am admired by others. God should be the sole witness of the good that I do. God knows the true intentions of my heart and will reward me accordingly.

To Consider

- How can I witness to my faith without appearing arrogant or self-righteous?
- What practical application can I give to the three penitential disciplines of Lent—prayer, fasting, and almsgiving?

To Pray

Lord Jesus, be my guide as I begin this Lenten journey. Help me to follow your example by doing everything for the love of God and neighbor.

Thursday after Ash Wednesday

Lk 9:22–25
   Deut 30:15–20; Ps 1

If any want to become my followers, let them deny
themselves and take up their cross daily and follow me.
— Lk 9:23

To Note

The Sign of the Cross is a sacramental symbol of our
salvation. Touching the forehead, we entrust our
lives to the Father. Placing a hand on the breast, we
commit our hearts to the Son. Touching each shoul-
der, we pray for the grace of the Holy Spirit to give
us strength to live the gospel.

To Understand

Moses offers the people a choice: life and prosperity
or death and doom. Following God's way brings
blessings. Going the other way brings a curse.
"Choose life," Moses exhorts, "that you may live!"
Jesus seems to turn this concept upside down. Although no one followed God's way more closely than
Jesus, he endured suffering, rejection, and was put
to death. At the time of Jesus, the people were
waiting in hope for a political Messiah, one who
would liberate them from all their foreign oppressors
and return the nation to its former might. Jesus
refuses the way of power and glory. His way is the

way of the cross. Jesus lays down the conditions for discipleship. All who wish to follow him must imitate his example by practicing self-denial and patiently enduring the trials of life. They must be willing to proclaim the gospel with faith despite rejection. A disciple must let go of earthly rewards for the sake of the gospel. Although the choice is a hard one, following Jesus does bring blessings. When we choose to follow him, we reject death and doom. We choose the gift of eternal life.

To Consider

- What does carrying the cross mean to me?
- Do I choose to carry it or is it forced upon me?
- What difference will it make if I refuse to carry the cross?

To Pray

Lord Jesus, give me the strength to take another step as I follow you day by day. Help me to bear my cross with grace.

Friday after Ash Wednesday

Mt 9:14–15
  Isa 58:1–9; Ps 51

The days will come when the bridegroom is taken away
from them, and then they will fast. — Mt 9:15

To Note

The Jewish practice of fasting was adopted by the
early church (Acts 13:2). Fasting was done to control
one's appetite for the things of the world in order to
hunger for spiritual things. Our Lenten fast should
represent our desire to grow spiritually as we hunger
for Jesus' presence in the Eucharist, and for his
appearance at the end of time.

To Understand

Isaiah tells the people to raise their voices like a
trumpet blast against injustice. He brings them face
to face with their hypocrisy. "Is this the manner of
fasting God wants?" the prophet demands. "Bowing
one's head and wearing sackcloth and ashes—do you
call that a fast? Is that acceptable to the Lord?" He
tells them to look around at those who are bound
unjustly. Isaiah's words sound timely. Share your
bread with the hungry! Shelter the homeless! Cloth
the naked! Don't turn your back on those who are
suffering. Jesus echoes these words hundreds of
years later in his sermon on the final judgment (Mt

25). Those who recognize the suffering Christ in the world's unfortunate ones will be eternally blessed by God. When the followers of John the Baptist ask Jesus why he and his disciples do not fast, Jesus uses Isaiah's image of a marriage to describe his relationship with his church (Is 54:5–7). While Jesus, the bridegroom, is among his people, it is a time for celebration because the sick are healed and the oppressed are set free. When Jesus is taken away, then the people will grieve and fast.

To Consider

- What aspects of my life do I need to get under control this Lent?
- How will this help me to hunger for spiritual realities?
- What can I share with the needy?

To Pray

Lord Jesus, help me to hunger for justice in this world. Help me to share my goods with those who are in need.

Saturday after Ash Wednesday

Lk 5:27–32
    Isa 58:9–14; Ps 86

> *I have come to call not the righteous to repentance but*
> *sinners to repentance. — Lk 5:32*

To Note

The Latin word *conversio* means a turning point. A conversion is a change from unbelief to belief, turning from a sinful path toward a new life in Christ. Since Vatican II, the term is not used to describe a non-Catholic Christian who becomes a Catholic. The preferred expression is "entering into full communion with the church."

To Understand

"God, you're so lucky to have me skip a meal or two for you," the self-righteous boast about their fasting. The prophet tells them to stop thinking that God will reward them for their piety. True fasting means aligning oneself with the poor and suffering. "Remove oppression!" the prophet cries. "Bestow your bread on the hungry! Satisfy the afflicted!" Then the dark world will be filled with glorious light, and the parched land will overflow with plenty. Jesus came to reveal God's mercy, but he is criticized for associating with the rejects of society. Tax collectors were among the outcasts because extortion and greed were often associated with their office. They were also despised as traitors since they worked for the Roman government. Jesus accepts people as they are. He invites a tax collector named Levi ("Matthew" in Mt 9:9) to abandon his post and follow him as a disciple. In gratitude, Levi gives a banquet in Jesus' honor. When Jesus is criticized for keeping company with these public sinners, he says that he has not come for those who think they have it all together, but for those who humbly recognize their need to change their lives.

To Consider

- What turning point or cross-road do I face in my life?
- Which direction will I take?
- Will my choice offer opportunity or danger?

To Pray

Lord Jesus, help me to be open to your call even when it means great changes in my life. Give me the grace to respond with joy.

First Sunday of Lent (ABC)

(A) Mt 4:1–11
   Gen 2:7–9, 3:1–7, Ps 51, Rom 5:12–19
(B) Mk 1:12-15
   Gen 9:8-15; Ps 25; 1 Pet 3:18-22
(C) Lk 4:1-13
   Deut 26:4-10; Ps 91; Rom 10:8-13

He was in the wilderness forty days, tempted by Satan.
— Mk 1:13

To Note

The Rite of Election, or Enrollment of Names, marks the final stage of the catechumenate. The catechumens preparing for baptism and the candidates seeking full incorporation into the church are sent forth to be recognized by the bishop. All the faithful have the opportunity to express their approval and support.

To Understand

Israel's stories summon us to hear our own stories of sin and grace. In the story of Adam and Eve, we see the personification of the human race. When we collaborate with evil, evil ends up destroying us. The consequence of sin is alienation, war, racism, crime, drugs, and death. We break our relationship with God when we have been given everything we need yet we say we don't have enough. When we become grasping and self-seeking, we are driven out of "paradise" so that we can learn the lesson of the desert. In the desert we hunger and thirst and begin to understand that we cannot live "on bread alone" but on God's word, which is always near us, even on our lips and in our hearts. When we face our weakness, admit our faults and addictions, then God can deliver us with an "outstretched arm." Like Noah, we are saved by God's mercy and grace. In the waters of baptism, we realize that everyone who calls on the name of the Lord will be saved. Jesus is the new Adam, who unites himself with sinful humanity, a "just man for the sake of the unjust," immersing himself in our sinfulness so that we can become sons and daughters of God. Jesus is the new Moses, who brings us to a "land flowing with milk and honey." Jesus tells us to reform our lives and believe the good news. The time of fulfillment is at hand!

To Consider

• How has the Lord assisted me in my desert wanderings?
• How has God's word helped me to resist evil and do good?

To Pray

Lord Jesus, I reject Satan, and all his works and empty promises, so that I might live in the freedom of God's children (Renewal of Baptismal Promises).

Monday of First Week of Lent

Mt 25:31–46
  Lev 19:1–2,11–18; Ps 19

Truly I tell you, just as you did it to one of the least of these who are members of my family, you did it to me.
— *Mt 25:40*

To Note

In the Hebrew Scriptures, the Day of the Lord was to be one of judgment and cosmic destruction (Joel 3:1–5). For Christians, the last judgment takes place at the Parousia, or final coming of Christ, when humanity will be judged according to the corporal works of mercy toward the hungry, lonely, homeless, poor, sick, dying, and imprisoned.

To Understand

"Be holy, for I, Yahweh, your God, am holy" (Lev 19:2). The way we can imitate divine holiness is found in God's commands: don't lie, cheat, steal, or hate. Forgive. Don't slander or take revenge against those who offend you. Render impartial justice toward both the weak and strong. The psalmist says that even the simple can understand the wisdom of God's law, which is trustworthy, clear and true. Jesus teaches us that God's holiness is revealed by the way we love our neighbors. He gives us a graphic metaphor for God's judgment of the righteous and the wicked in his parable of the sheep and goats. Jesus draws his comparison from the way these animals were pastured together during the day, then separated at nightfall. The criterion for God's judgment is the love that has been shown to the least ones: the poor, alienated, sick, and oppressed. The "sheep" are those who obeyed the shepherd's voice and responded with compassion. Because they recognized the suffering Christ in the world's unfortunate ones, they are given a favored place in the kingdom. The "goats" failed to heed his commands and are punished for their failure to do good.

To Consider

- What meaning does the word holiness have for modern Christians?
- How am I able to see Christ in the suffering and afflicted?
- What makes this difficult?

To Pray

Lord Jesus, help me to see you in all those who are in need. Help me to avoid evil by doing good.

Tuesday of First Week of Lent

Mt 6:7–15
    Isa 55:10–11; Ps 34

Your Father knows what you need before you ask him.
— Mt 6:8

To Note

Prayer has been described as lifting the mind and
heart to God. Prayer takes many forms—adoration,
praise, thanksgiving, contrition, or petition. Our
prayers can be vocal or mental, private or public. We
can pray for ourselves and for others, for the living
and for the dead. Faithfulness to prayer should have
a primary place in each of our lives.

To Understand

The prophet Isaiah writes from captivity in Babylon.
He knows that even in that remote corner of the
earth, God can hear his cries for mercy. Isaiah can
seek God whether he is in the sacred temple of
Jerusalem or far away in exile. God's response is as
inevitable as the rain and snow that waters the seed
beneath the crusty earth and makes it fertile. God's
word is as full of promise as the wheat that is ground
and baked into bread to satisfy the hungry. God's
word has a power and life of its own. Once spoken,
it cannot be called back. It goes forth to achieve its
intended purpose. Jesus says that the words we

speak to God have a power too. Once spoken they are certain to reach their destination. In fact, God hears them even before they are uttered. God is a loving parent who knows our daily need for bread, for forgiveness, for deliverance from oppression. We don't need many words, just a sincere desire to do God's will and to trust that we will be delivered from all that holds us captive.

To Consider

- When have I felt that God heard my prayers?
- When have my prayers gone unanswered?
- What helps me to trust that God will deliver me or my loved ones?

To Pray

God of the universe, Father of us all, help me to do your will so that your kingdom of peace and justice will reign. Help me to forgive others just as you have shown mercy to me.

Wednesday of First Week of Lent

Lk 11:29–32
    Jon 3:1–10; Ps 51

*Just as Jonah became a sign to the people of Nineveh, so
the Son of Man will be to this generation. — Lk 11:30*

To Note

The Vatican II Declaration on the Relation of the
Church to Non-Christian Religions urges her sons
and daughters to witness to their own "faith and way
of life" and to "acknowledge, preserve and encourage the spiritual and moral truths" found among all
peoples (#2). The church reproves any "discrimination against people or any harassment of them on the
basis of their race, color, condition in life, or religion"
(#5).

To Understand

The book of Jonah is the kind of story that can be
told around a camp fire. It has all the important
ingredients of a good novel: conflict, suspense, in-
trigue, fidelity and unfaithfulness. But it is more
than just a whale of a tale. It has the capacity to jar
us out of our complacency and narrow-mindedness.
The story reminds us that God's love and forgiveness are not limited to a particular group of people
(usually ourselves). God's mercy is offered to anyone
who desires to do what is right, even our enemies on

the other side of the world. Jonah tried to run away from that kind of God. But God wouldn't let him get away with it. Jonah was delivered to the very people he sought to avoid, the hated Ninevites in Assyria. Jesus said that we can't pretend that we are any better than Jonah. We too are an "evil generation" that prefers a religion of signs and wonders to one that makes moral demands of us. Those people of Nineveh, or whoever else we despise because they are not like us, will sit in judgment of all who hear Jesus' exhortation to change our lives but avoid doing anything about it.

To Consider

- When have I been like Jonah, running away from something God wants me to do?
- What is my attitude toward people who are different from myself?
- How can I grow in my understanding of them?

To Pray

Loving God, open my eyes to my self-righteous attitude that refuses to see all people as your children. Help me to repent of my prejudice and intolerance.

Thursday of First Week of Lent

Mt 7:7–12
  Esth C*:12,14–16,23–25; Ps 138

> *Ask, and it will be given you; search, and you will find;*
> *knock, and the door will be opened for you. — Mt 7:7*

To Note

The Book of Esther is read on the Feast of Purim.
The alleged origin of this post-exilic feast is the
deliverance of the Jews in Persia from Haman, the
first "Hitler," who attempted the genocide of the
Jewish people. The name of the feast is derived from
the casting of *pur* or lots to determine the day of the
extermination (Esth 3:7, 9:24).

To Understand

Esther is a story of reversal of fortunes. Esther, a
young Jewess in the harem of the king, supplants the
Queen of Persia. Haman, the king's vizier, plots to
annihilate the Jews and ends up on the very gallows
he intended for his victims. Queen Esther is willing
to put her own life on the line by pleading with the
king for the lives of her people, but first she seeks
divine assistance. She takes off her royal clothing and
puts on the garments of distress and mourning. Then
she beseeches God, her Lord and King, to deliver

---

* *The letters A–F signify Greek additions to the Hebrew text.*

her people. Jesus reminds us how important it is to come to God in prayer. He tells us to be persistent. Those who ask will receive. Those who seek will find. Those who knock will enter the abode of God's merciful heart. If human parents, with all their short-comings, can satisfy the needs of their children, how much more will God, their heavenly Father, give good things to those who ask. These good things may not be the ones we count on; nevertheless, God responds to our needs with love and compassion. In the same way, we are to obey the Golden Rule of doing the good things for others that we expect for ourselves.

To Consider

- Who are the oppressed people of today who need my intercessory prayers?
- When is it hardest for me to pray?
- What helps me to be persistent in prayer?

To Pray

Heavenly Father, help me to recognize your answers to my prayers. Help me to trust in your mercy for all who suffer injustice.

Friday of First Week of Lent

Mt 5:20–26
    Ezek 18:21–28; Ps 130

*First be reconciled to your brother or sister, and then
come and offer your gift. — Mt 5:24*

To Note

The word *metanoia* literally means "to change your
mind." It means seeing your former behavior in a
different light. A conscious decision to act according
to this new perception is the meaning of repentance.

To Understand

"God's not fair!" the people cried when they suffered the consequences of their actions. Ezekiel tells
them that they were complacent to think their past
virtues would make up for their sins. They can't
blame society or their parents or their teachers for
the wrong that they did. God holds each person
accountable if they break faith. The psalmist asks,
"If you mark iniquities, Lord, who can stand?"
Ezekiel says there is hope if the people repent of
their destructive ways. God takes no pleasure from
the downfall of those who do evil. Jesus also admon-
ishes those who give lip-service to God's law. While
the religious leaders advocated minute observance
of the law, their hearts were not committed to God's
will. Jesus expands the literal interpretation of the

law. To enter God's kingdom, one must go beyond outward acts of holiness by being charitable in all our actions. Jesus deepens the meaning of the law. Godliness must penetrate one's inner being and manifest itself in love and forgiveness. Jesus condemns murder, but also the thoughts, words and deeds that can kill. Anyone who has abused another must first go and be reconciled with that person before coming to worship God.

To Consider

- Do I obey church laws out of obligation or personal conviction?
- What religious acts do I perform by rote?
- What can I do to give them more meaning?

To Pray

Lord Jesus, give me a willingness to have my heart changed. Help me to take the necessary steps to reconcile myself with those whom I have offended.

Saturday of First Week of Lent

Mt 5:43–48
Deut 26:16–19; Ps 119

*Love your enemies and pray for those who persecute
you. — Mt 5:44*

To Note

The United States Bishop's Pastoral Statement on
war and peace states: "Because peace, like the Kingdom of God itself, is both a divine gift and a human
work, the church should continually pray for the gift
and share in the work. We are called to be a church
at the service of peace" ("The Challenge of Peace:
God's Promise and Our Response," 1983).

To Understand

Moses told Israel that they were a peculiar people.
Moses probably meant "singular," not "odd," but
the fact remains that the human race is rather curious. Though made in the divine image and called to
be holy, we often act ungodly and unholy. We hear
God's law as a prescription for unity and peace, but
we make a feeble attempt to obey it. We have not
taken the law into our hearts and allowed it to transform us into the kind of people God intends. God
wants us to walk in the way of divine justice with all
our hearts and souls. "Happy are they who follow the
law of the Lord," the psalmist says. Jesus doesn't let

us off the hook either. In fact, he demands that his followers go beyond the ordinary standards of behavior and act extraordinarily. Jesus says that you don't have to be a Christian to love those who respect and admire you. Since God's love is unconditional, Jesus expects his disciples to be perfect by loving those who are spiteful and hateful. That seems like an impossible demand for imperfect human beings. St. Bernard tells us that perfection is a sincere attempt to progress and increase in virtue. That gives us peculiar people a better chance to be perfect.

To Consider

- How can I love someone who has mistreated me?
- Is this the same as being a doormat?
- What steps must I take to be reconciled with someone?

To Pray

Lord Jesus, help me to be merciful and forgiving, and to show your love to those who have injured me. Help me to work for peace and justice in all I say and do.

Second Sunday of Lent (ABC)

(A) Mt 17:1–9
   Gen 12:1–4; Ps 33; 2 Tim 1:8–10
(B) Mk 9:2–10
   Gen 22:1–2,9,10–13,15–18; Ps 116; Rom 8:31–34
(C) Lk 9:28–36
   Gen 15:5–12,17–18; Ps 27; Phil 3:17–4:1

This is my Son the Beloved; with him I am well pleased;
listen to him! — Mt 17:5

To Note

Lent is an intense spiritual journey for the elect who
are preparing for baptism. Baptism is no mere symbolic ceremony; it represents our daily dying and
rising with Christ. Lent is an opportunity for each of
us to become more aware of our own baptismal
calling and to renew our commitment to be faithful
to Christ and his church.

To Understand

In the story of Abraham's call, we hear an invitation
to be obedient and faithful to the Lord's call in our
own lives. Abraham's relationship with God was a
sacred partnership, a covenant that confirmed his
identity as a member of God's people. Abraham's
fidelity was tested when God asked him to offer his
only son Isaac as a holocaust. At the last moment,
God stays Abraham's hand and provides the sacrifice.

Because Abraham trusted in God's direction, he showed himself to be a true son of God. Paul reminds his beloved "son" Timothy that Christ saved him from the power of death and has called him to a new life of holiness and fidelity. Paul consoles those who are enduring doubt and suffering: "If God is for us, who can be against us?" If God provided the sacrifice for our sins, allowing Jesus to die for the sake of us all, will God not grant all things besides?

The transfiguration is a timeless message of faith and trust in the midst of affliction. As Jesus faces death on Calvary, he shows his disciples what sonship is all about. On the mountaintop they behold Jesus' future glory in the company of Moses and Elijah, two great figures from the first covenant. Out of the darkness, a shaft of light is seen, and a voice confirms that Jesus is the chosen Son of the new covenant. When we listen to Jesus, we prove ourselves to be faithful sons and daughters of God.

To Consider

- Am I able to see light in the midst of darkness?
- Am I able to say with Paul, "Be imitators of me" in moments of distress?

To Pray

Lord Jesus, help me to be faithful to my baptismal covenant as I face the trials of life. Strengthen me as I journey with you.

Monday of Second Week of Lent

Lk 6:36–38
   Dan 9:4–10; Ps 79

Be merciful, just as your Father is merciful. — Lk 6:36

To Note

Vatican II Pastoral Constitution on the Church in the Modern World states: "God alone is the judge and the searcher of hearts: (God) forbids us to pass judgment on the inner guilt of others. The teaching of Christ demands that we forgive injury, and the precept of love, which is the commandment of the New Law, includes all our enemies" (#28).

To Understand

Daniel doesn't look around for someone to blame for the evil in his world. He accuses everyone, including himself. "We have sinned." "We have rebelled." "We have not obeyed." Everyone—kings, princes, parents, all the people of the land—have refused to listen to the message of the prophets who tried to warn them of the consequences of their actions. Daniel says that everyone should be shamefaced before the Lord, yet he has faith in a compassionate God to forgive them. Jesus also tells his followers not to point the finger at someone else. His commands to them are clear: "Be compassionate!" "Do not judge!" "Do not condemn!" "Forgive!" "Give!" In

Matthew's gospel, Jesus says that since their heavenly Father is perfect, his disciples should be perfect (Mt 5:48). That's pretty intimidating for ordinary folk. In Luke's gospel, God's mercy is stressed rather than perfection. Jesus' disciples are children of a compassionate Father; therefore, they must wholeheartedly imitate this divine mercy. Since God forgives their sins, they should pardon the faults of others. God cannot be outdone in generosity. Because Jesus' disciples have shown tolerance and charity toward others, God will shower them with abundant blessings.

To Consider

- Am I able to pray, "Forgive me my faults as I forgive those who injure me"?
- Am I trying to fix someone else's behavior, or am I trying to correct my own faults this Lent?

To Pray

Lord God, teach me to be compassionate, loving, generous and kind. Thank you for showing mercy to me.

Tuesday of Second Week of Lent

Mt 23:1–12
  Isa 1:10,16–20; Ps 50

> *All who exalt themselves will be humbled, and all who*
> *humble themselves will be exalted. — Mt 23:12*

To Note

The Vatican II "Decree on the Ministry and Life of
Priests" states that humility and obedience are special spiritual requirements of the "true minister of
Christ" who is advised to be "conscious of his own
weakness and to labor in humility." The will of God,
who sent him, will be carried out "by humbly placing
himself at the service of all those who are entrusted
to his care by God" (#15).

To Understand

Isaiah looks at Israel to the north and Judah to the
south and he doesn't like what he sees in either
direction. "Remove the evil of your doings from
before my eyes" (Isa 1:16), he says. Isaiah warns the
people that their worship is phony and empty because they have closed their eyes and ears to the
pleas of the poor and helpless. The prophet's remedy
is simple: "Wash yourself clean!" By making justice
their goal, their scarlet sins will become white as
snow. The psalmist picks up this theme. God isn't
blind and deaf to our guilt. God corrects us by draw-

ing up our sins before our eyes. Jesus points out the way we close our eyes to sin by pretending to be something different from what we really are. The word for this is "hypocrite!" Jesus directs his complaint to the religious leaders whose complicated interpretation of the law laid a heavy yoke on the backs of the people. He advises the people to pay attention to what these teachers say, but not to blindly follow their example—because their deeds didn't agree with their words. While these prideful leaders loved to call attention to their piety by the external trappings and titles of their office, they refused to lift a finger to lighten the load of the people. Jesus reminds them that God is the true teacher, master and Father of them all. God will exalt those who humbly acknowledge their sinfulness.

To Consider

- Am I blind to my faults?
- Am I hypocritical about the religious acts I perform?
- Do I aim to serve God or to be honored and respected by others?

To Pray

Lord Jesus, turn my eyes toward God and away from my self-centeredness. Help me to see you in those I serve.

Wednesday of Second Week of Lent

Mt 20:17–28
    Jer 18:18–20; Ps 31

*Whoever wishes to be great among you must be your
servant. — Mt 20:26*

To Note

The Dogmatic Constitution on the Church declares
that "Christ is the great prophet who proclaimed the
kingdom of the Father both by the testimony of his
life and by the power of his word." It further states
that "this prophetic office" is shared "not only by the
hierarchy...but also by the laity" who should not
hide their hope but give witness to it through their
lives (35).

To Understand

There aren't many perks to being a prophet—no sick
benefits, paid holidays, or vacations. A prophet is one
who stands against the status quo of society and
speaks God's mind despite the consequences. Not
many wanted to be on the prophet's side. That might
mean alienation from friends and family, loss of em-
ployment, and even loss of one's life. Jeremiah re-
lates another plot against his life. His enemies could
have been from the establishment, the priests, sages
and official court prophets, who wanted to prove that
Jeremiah's teaching about them deserved the death

penalty. The establishment usually defends the establishment. As Jesus journeys toward Jerusalem and the cross, he takes his apostles aside and tells them that he will be handed over to the religious leaders who will condemn him to death. The apostles are incredulous. That's no way to treat the Messiah! The mother of James and John mirrors their skepticism. She ignores the issue and asks Jesus if he wouldn't mind giving her sons special places of honor in the kingdom. The other apostles are indignant. (Did they wish they had thought of it first?) Jesus teaches them that his role is not one of power but of service. His path to glory is through humble submission to the will of God. If his followers want to be truly great, they must offer their lives for the sake of others.

To Consider

- Are my motives for Christian service self-serving?
- Do I serve for personal reward or do I work for peace and justice in the world?

To Pray

Lord Jesus rescue me from the snares of prestige and power. Help me to commit myself to your service.

Thursday of Second Week of Lent

Lk 16:19–31
  Jer 17:5–10; Ps 1

If they do not listen to Moses and the prophets, neither will they be convinced even if someone rises from the dead. — Lk 16:31

To Note

In their document "Economic Justice for All" (1986), the United States Bishops stated that in view of the widespread poverty that still afflicts the greater part of the world, there must be a "preferential option for the poor." The suffering and needy should have the most urgent claim on the conscience of the nation and the church.

To Understand

The prophet Jeremiah knows that there are those seeking his life. He cannot trust those whose hearts are turned from God. Only God can assist him. The psalmist's reasoning is similar. Don't heed the counsel of the wicked. Only those who have a genuine relationship with God can be depended upon. Jesus tells a parable that contrasts the wicked and virtuous. He addresses it to the self-righteous well-to-do who paid no attention to the poor who lay sick and dying right on their doorsteps. The protagonists in the drama are a wealthy man at the top of the social ladder and a poor man at the bottom. The scene is set in the rich man's house where he dines in sumptuous luxury (Mmm-good!). Outside his door lies Lazarus, starving and covered with sores (Yuck!). But there is a reversal of fortunes when the two men die. Lazarus is taken to the bosom of Abraham, the abode of the righteous (Mmm-good!). The rich man lands in the netherworld where he is in torment (Yuck!). The rich man begs Father Abraham to send Lazarus to help him. Abraham explains that a great gulf separates the two that cannot be crossed. The rich man then pleads for someone to warn his family of the terrible fate that awaits them. Abraham says that if they have not listened to the prophets, they won't believe anyone else, even if that person should rise from the dead.

To Consider

- Do I recognize the plight of the suffering in my community?
- What is my parish doing for the poor, sick and dying?
- Who is the Lazarus in my life whom I have ignored?

To Pray

Lord Jesus, open my eyes and ears to the abused, scorned and suffering people around me. Help me to see you in all those I serve.

Friday of Second Week of Lent

Mt 21:33–43,45–46
    Gen 37:3–4,12–13,17–28; Ps 105

The stone that the builders rejected has become the
cornerstone. — Mt 21:42

To Note

The seven capital sins are pride, greed, anger, envy,
lust, gluttony, and sloth. They are called cardinal sins
because they are the source of all other sin. They are
also deadly sins because they can lead to mortal sin.

To Understand

"Here comes that master dreamer," Joseph's brothers said to one another. "Come on, let's kill him!"
said one. "Let's just throw him down a well," suggested another. "Let's sell him to the traders and
make money off the deal," said a third. Envy, anger,
greed—sins that can lead to murder—are directed at
their own flesh and blood. The account of Joseph,
loved by his father and forsaken by his brothers, is a
story that prefigures Jesus, who is scorned by the
ones to whom he is sent. Jesus addresses a parable to
the religious leaders who will reject him and put him
to death. In his parable of the vineyard, Jesus recalls
Isaiah's "Song of the Vineyard" that allegorizes
God's saving work (Isa 5:1–7). In the story, God is
the owner of a vineyard (the chosen people of Israel).

Before going on a journey, the owner leases the vineyard to tenants (the religious leaders), leaving it in their care. At harvest time (the messianic era), the owner sends his servants (the prophets) to see what fruits (good works) have been produced. The tenants seize the servants and beat them. Then the owner sends his own son (Christ), thinking that the tenants will respect him. But they kill him, laying claim to the land. Because these leaders have failed to recognize the one God sent to them, others (the Gentiles), will benefit from God's mercy, and they will yield a rich harvest.

To Consider

- Do the sins of anger, jealousy, or greed hinder my work for the Lord?
- How do I treat the people that God sends to challenge me?
- When am I called to speak God's message to those in authority?

To Pray

Lord Jesus, help me to root out the sins that prevent me from growing good fruit in my life.

Saturday of Second Week of Lent

Lk 15:1–3,11–32
  Mic 7:14–15,18–20; Ps 103

*This son of mine was dead and is alive again; he was
lost and is found.* — *Lk 15:24*

To Note

Since Vatican II, the new name for confession is the
"Order of Penance" or the "Rite of Reconciliation."
The rite has been revised to more clearly express the
nature and effects of the sacrament, to emphasize its
relationship to the community, and to place confession and absolution in the context of a celebration of
the word of God.

To Understand

In no uncertain terms, Micah denounces the widespread corruption in both Samaria and Judea. The
prophet leaves no one out—merchants, judges,
priests, and prophets all come under his attack for
their apostasy. In contrast, the Lord has remained
faithful to the covenant. Micah prays for national
restoration and trusts in God's mercy to pardon their
sins.

Nowhere in scripture are God's kindness and mercy
toward sinners better expressed than in the story of
the prodigal son. The younger son in the story bla-

tantly demands his inheritance: "I can't sit around and wait for you to die, so give it to me now!" After squandering everything, the son realizes the error of his ways and heads toward home. Humbled, he no longer sees himself as a son, but as a servant in his father's household. Before he reaches his destination, the young man sees his father running down the road to joyfully greet him. The father restores him to sonship and celebrates his return with a banquet. The elder son refuses to recognize the younger son as his brother. Neither does he see himself as a son but as a slave for his father all these years. "My son," says the father tenderly, "everything I have belongs to you, but we must celebrate! This brother of yours was dead and has come back to life. He was lost and now he is found."

To Consider

- Which character in the story do I recognize as myself?
- Have I seen the pattern of sin, forgiveness and celebration in my life?
- How can I relate this to the sacramental life of the church?

To Pray

Merciful Father, give me the grace to seek forgiveness of those whom I have injured and to forgive those who have offended me.

Third Sunday of Lent (ABC)

(A) Jn 4:5–42
   Ex 17:3–7; Ps 95; Rom 5:1–2,5–8
(B) Jn 2:13–25
   Ex 20:1–17; Ps 19; 1 Cor 1:22–25
(C) Lk 13:1–9
   Ex 3:1–8,13–15; Ps 103; 1 Cor 10:1–6,10–12

Those who drink of the water that I will give them will never be thirsty. — Jn 4:14

To Note

The scrutinies are important rituals celebrated with the elect on the third, fourth and fifth Sundays in Lent in preparation for baptism. The A Cycle of readings is used in these rites. The scrutinies are meant to uncover and heal anything that blocks God's love from being poured out in the hearts of the elect. We are all encouraged to examine our own thirsts for power, prestige, and possessions.

To Understand

Water is a powerful symbol for people living in the arid desert. In the Bible, water signifies thirsting for God and being cleansed from sin. God saved the Israelites from slavery by their passage through the sea into freedom. Having freed them, God shows them how to remain free. Having taken them out of an unjust society, God reveals how they can live in peace and justice with God and one another by obeying the covenant. In the desert, Moses witnessed a manifestation of God's mercy. God's self-revelation was "I am who I am"—not an abstract deity but eternally present and personally involved in people's lives. During Israel's forty-year journey through the desert, the people were often dissatisfied, and they grumbled against God and Moses. Despite their unfaithfulness, God pours out love, refreshes them in the wilderness and brings them to the promised land.

Jesus comes to replace old institutions that were no longer life-giving with the new covenant of God's love. Jesus is the new temple of God's everlasting presence. Jesus describes this presence with the symbol of water. This is no ordinary water but the living water of the Spirit that springs up from within us. Jesus reminds us that we cannot presume on God's mercy. We must turn to God and reform our lives while we have the opportunity.

To Consider

- In what ways am I spiritually dry?
- Am I thirsting for the things of God this Lent?
- Have I taken the time to repent of my transgressions?

To Pray

Lord Jesus, help me to always thirst for God. Let me drink deeply from the well of your life-giving Spirit.

Monday of Third Week of Lent

Lk 4:24–30
  2 Kings 5:1–15; Ps 42

No prophet is accepted in the prophet's hometown.
— Lk 4:24

To Note

The presentation of the Creed to the elect is celebrated in the third Week of Lent. The Apostle's
Creed is so-called because it is a summary of apostolic teaching. The Nicene Creed used in the liturgy
was issued by the Council of Nicaea in 325 CE*, and
was further developed by the Council of Constantinople in 381 CE. The Creed reminds us all to bear
witness to our faith throughout our lives.

To Understand

Naaman was a respected army commander in Syria,
but he also had leprosy. "Go to Elisha!" a little Israeli
slave girl had faith that the prophet could cure her
master. "Go to Israel!" the king of Aram told
Naaman. Naaman expected Elisha to simply wave
his hand and he would be healed, but the prophet

---

* *"CE" is an abbreviations for "Common Era," a term that
corresponds to "AD" or* Anno Domine, *the Year of the Lord.
"CE" is a religiously neutral term that respects Jews and other
non-Christians.*

told Naaman to do something ridiculous. "Go and wash seven times in the river Jordan and you will be healed." The commander was angry. Why had he come all this way? The rivers back in Syria were broad and clear while the river Jordan was narrow and muddy. Naaman's servant persuaded him to give it a try even if it seemed foolish. When Naaman came out of the water, his flesh was like that of a newborn. Naaman testified to his faith in the God of Israel. Israel's rivers might not be superior to Syria's, but their God was. Jesus compares the faith of this pagan to that of his own people. He says that there were many lepers in Israel at the time of Elisha, but it was a foreigner who had faith and was healed. Like the prophets before him, Jesus' own people refuse to believe in him and they attempt to kill him. Because they have rejected the one who had been sent to them, others will benefit from God's mercy .

To Consider

- Do I bear witness to my faith in Jesus?
- Have I experienced rejection because of this?
- Who are today's prophets whose message is ignored?

To Pray

Lord Jesus, my soul is thirsting for you. Wash me clean with your life-giving words.

Tuesday of Third Week of Lent

Mt 18:21–35
  Dan 3:25,34–43; Ps 25

Lord, if another member of the church sins against me,
how often should I forgive? — Mt 18:21

To Note

Contrition for sin is an act of worship. Perfect contrition has as its motive faith and love of God. Imperfect contrition is the fear of God's punishment. An act of contrition is required for the remission of sin. True contrition must express grief and detestation of sin, a resolve to avoid sin in the future, and a determination to make amends accordingly.

To Understand

"Shadrach, Meshach, and Abednego" is the name of an old spiritual. These are also the names of three heroes of faith who suffered at the hands of Antiochus IV Epiphanes, the worst of the Seleucid kings. To protect himself from persecution, the author of the book of Daniel places his story back in the days of another tyrant, the Babylonian King Nebuchadnezzar. Any Israelite could read between the lines and know who the current villain was. The song of the three youths in the fiery furnace is a prayer of contrition. Abednego prays with a contrite heart and humble spirit that they might be offered up as holocausts for the sins that brought their nation low. Jesus teaches that forgiveness of others is a requirement for being forgiven oneself. When Peter asks how often he must forgive a fellow disciple who has offended him, Jesus says that forgiveness must be without limit (seven was regarded as a perfect number). Then he tells a story of a master who forgives his servant a huge debt that the man had no way of repaying. Yet the same servant refuses to forgive a fellow servant a much smaller sum owed him. Jesus says that God's mercy toward us will correspond to our own willingness to extend forgiveness to others.

To Consider

- Whom do I find it hardest to forgive—a stranger, a neighbor, or a family member?
- What steps do I need to take today to forgive someone?

To Pray

Lord God, grant me the grace to forgive those who have hurt me. The mercy I offer others is just a shadow of your mercy toward me.

Wednesday of Third Week of Lent

Mt 5:17–19
   Deut 4:1,5–9; Ps 147

Do not think I have come to abolish the law or the
prophets; I have come not to abolish but to fulfill.
— Mt 5:17

To Note

Conscience is a personal judgment regarding the
rightness or wrongness of a deed. Conscience affects
the will in a course of action. Although one cannot be
forced to go against the guiding principles of one's
conscience, everyone must strive to form a right
conscience according to faith and reason.

To Understand

After years of slavery in Egypt, and more years wan-
dering in the wilderness, Moses prepares the people
to enter the land God promised to Abraham and his
descendants. Moses recalls the fidelity of God, who
saved them, and prays that once they occupy the
land, the people will observe the decrees God has
commanded. Moses urges the people never to forget
the mighty things God has done in their midst, and
to teach them to their children and grandchildren. If
they are faithful to the law, everyone who hears of
God's justice will acclaim the wisdom of God's people. In his sermon on the Mount, Jesus is the new

Moses who comes to fulfill the law, not to abolish it. Jesus teaches his followers that the law has lasting validity. Even the smallest letter in the Hebrew alphabet (*iota*) or a tiny flourish of the pen (*yod*) will not pass from the law. Jesus is the embodiment of God's law. Through his words and works, Jesus brings the law to perfection, raising it to higher standards, deepening its meaning and widening its application. Those who follow him must be grounded in his teaching and teach others according to God's will. Those who are faithful to God's law will inherit a place in God's kingdom. Those who willfully disregard it will be excluded.

To Consider

- In what ways do my words and actions give good examples of my belief in God's law?
- How do I teach others to respect God's commands?
- Which of God's laws is the most neglected today?

To Pray

Lord God, help me to witness to the truth of your law. Help me to reflect Christ's love and justice in all I say and do.

Thursday of Third Week of Lent

Lk 11:14–23
  Jer 7:23–28; Ps 95

> *If Satan also is divided against himself, how will his kingdom stand? — Lk 11:18*

To Note

One of the rites of baptism is the Ephphetha Rite, or the rite of opening ears, and mouth. By the power of its symbolism, the elect are impressed with their need for grace so that they may hear and proclaim God's saving word. All the faithful are reminded of their failure to profess the faith they hear.

To Understand

Jeremiah fares no better than the prophets throughout the ages who had warned the people of their misdeeds, but whose voices were not heeded. Jeremiah laments the spiritual condition of the people. Their backs are turned against God. Their faces are looking in another direction. Their feet are set on the wrong path. Their necks are stiffened in opposition to God's ways. Their hearts are hardened against God's law. Their ears are closed to God's message. Their lips no longer speak the word "faithfulness." Jesus comes to open hearts, eyes, ears and mouths so that the people might proclaim the wonders of God's mercy. Yet when he heals a man who was mute, some

46

refuse to believe that his power is from God. They accuse him of performing these miracles in the name of Beelzebul (a contemptuous term for Satan). Jesus points out the absurdity of the accusation. If Satan is using his power to cast out demons, then the evil one is working against himself and will be defeated. Jesus is the one mightier prophesied by John the Baptist (Lk 3:16), whose words and deeds will attack Satan's stronghold. All who unite with Jesus in his opposition to evil are helping to establish God's reign. Those who work against him are assisting the adversary who is attempting to destroy God's realm.

To Consider

- How have I heard God speak this week?
- In what ways have I seen God at work in my life?
- What evil conditions in society am I working to overcome?

To Pray

Lord Jesus, open my ears so that I might hear your voice in those around me. Open my mouth to proclaim your message of salvation.

Friday of Third Week of Lent

Mk 12:28–34
    Hos 14:2–10; Ps 81

There is no other commandment greater than these.
— Mk 12:31

To Note

"Torah" refers to the "law of Moses," the first five
books of the Bible. In its broad sense, Torah describes God's ongoing revelation as a guide to life.
Pharisaism defined the law as including 613 commandments of greater and lesser degree whose transgressions were more or less grave. Jesus says that
righteousness is attained by love and justice, the true
purpose of the law.

To Understand

Hosea delivers an invitation to a faithless people:
"Return to God, who loves you. God will forgive you
and take you back." Hosea was speaking from personal experience. His wife Gomer was adulterous,
yet he loved her and longed for her return. Hosea
compares his own misfortune with God's, whose
people had a love affair with false gods. Because
immorality had corroded the moral fiber of the people, they had abandoned the covenant with God in
favor of foreign alliances. When they began to suffer
the consequences for their sins, Hosea tells them

that God is compassionate. If they are contrite, God will pardon them and restore their former prosperity.

A scribe, a learned interpreter of the law of Israel, asks Jesus which law is the most important. Jesus reminds him of the great prayer of Israel, the Shema ("Hear!" Deut 6:4), which commanded the people to love God with their whole being—heart, soul, mind, and strength. The second command was based on the first: love of neighbor and love of self. On these principles, all the other laws stand. The scribe agrees that to love God, neighbor, and oneself is worth more than all the religious acts one can perform. By recognizing this truth, the scribe has moved a step closer to God's reign.

To Consider

- How do I demonstrate my love of God?
- How do I show my neighbors I love them?
- Do I love myself?

To Pray

Lord God, I want to love you with all my heart and soul, mind, and strength. Help me to share your love with others.

Saturday of Third Week of Lent

Lk 18:9–14
    Hos 6:1–6; Ps 51

God, be merciful to me, a sinner! — Lk 18:13

To Note

The Jesus Prayer is an ancient Christian prayer of the Eastern Desert Fathers. Like the Publican in the gospel, the prayer invokes the saving power of Jesus' name. To say the prayer, center on each phrase while breathing rhythmically: "Lord Jesus Christ" (breath in) "Son of God" (breath out) "have mercy" (breath in) "on me a sinner" (breath out).

To Understand

The prophet Hosea compares the people's faithfulness to an evaporating dew—present in the cool of the morning, then gone in the heat of day. In contrast, God's love is as certain as the dawn, as dependable as the spring rains. The people offer oblations to their false gods, but God asks only for love, not sacrifice. The psalmist says that a repentant spirit is worth more than all the holocausts one can offer in appeasement for sin. Jesus tells a parable about the need to approach God with a humble and contrite heart. He contrasts the self-righteous attitude of a Pharisee with that of a Publican. Publicans, or tax collectors, were regarded as sinners because of their collaboration with the occupying Roman government. Often they were accused of extorting money from their own people. The Pharisee thanks God that he is not like the rest of sinful humanity, especially the tax collector whom he holds in contempt. He sees himself as superior to others because he observes the law of fasts and tithes. The Pharisee prays with his head unbowed and does not even think of asking God to pardon his sins. On the other hand, the tax collector dares not raise his eyes to heaven as he humbly prays for God's forgiveness. Jesus declares that this man is justified before God because he repents of his sins and confesses his need for salvation.

To Consider

- Am I like the Pharisee in my attitude toward my own and other people's sins?
- Am I like the Publican, afraid to come before God with my sins?

To Pray

Pray the ancient Jesus Prayer: "Lord Jesus, Son of God, have mercy on me, a sinner."

Fourth Sunday in Lent (ABC)

(A) Jn 9:1–41
   1 Sam 16:1,6–7,10–13; Ps 23; Eph 5:8–14
(B) Jn 3:14–21
   2 Chr 36:14–17,19–23; Ps 137; Eph 2:4–10
(C) Lk 15:1–3,11–32
   Josh 5:9,10–12; Ps 34; 2 Cor 5:17–21

One thing I do know, that though I was blind, now I see. — Jn 9:25

To Note

The second of three scrutinies is celebrated with the elect on the fourth Sunday in Lent in preparation for baptism. The scrutiny is meant to uncover and heal any darkness in the hearts of the elect. The scrutinies encourage the faithful to examine their own spiritual blindness and prejudices and repent of these defects.

To Understand

In David's call, we can understand our own election. Although others might assume that we are undeserving, God scrutinizes the depths of our beings, and as with David, finds that each of is worthy and loved. God is a good shepherd who guides and corrects us, feeds and anoints us, forgives us our sins, and heals us. When Jesus sees a man who has been blind from birth, the people claim to have insights into Gods' ways. They say that the man's blindness is punishment for sin, but their blindness is worse than the man's. Jesus says that blindness is neither the man's fault nor anyone else's. In the healing of the blind man, God's glory shines forth, and he can see Jesus more clearly than those who could see all along. Jesus addresses a parable to us as a reminder of God's love for the wayward and lost. In the story, a son squanders all the gifts his father had given him. When the son realizes the error of his ways, he turns toward home. Before he can reach his destination, he discovers that his father is there waiting for his return. The elder brother in the story is each of us when we refuse to believe that God can change the hearts of those who have gone astray. Paul rejoices that in Christ we are a new creation because we have been reconciled to God. God did not send the Son to condemn us but to give us sight when we are blind and bring us to life when we are dead.

To Consider

- What blindness prevents me from seeing Jesus?
- Do I have a blind spot to my own faults?
- How am I blind to the needs of others?

To Pray

Lord Jesus, I know that sometimes I am blind. I want to see you in all the people and events in my life.

Monday of Fourth Week of Lent

Jn 4:43–54
> Isa 65:17–21; Ps 30

*The father realized that this was the very hour when
Jesus had said to him, "Your son will live." — Jn 4:53*

To Note

In biblical thought, a sign is a symbolic reminder of
the reality it signifies, proof that God acts and saves.
In the church, acts or objects that have particular
religious meaning are "signs." The sign of the cross,
the crucifix, the sacramentary, and the lectionary are
signs that direct our attention to the spiritual realities
they represent, symbols of our salvation.

To Understand

God continually recreates and redeems the world.
The prophet Isaiah imagines a new earth that will
eclipse God's former creation. The signs of this ideal
world are goals we can all strive toward: liberation
from suffering, injustice, or exploitation. The psalmist echoes this dream: "You changed my mourning
into dancing." Jesus comes to fulfill the prophet's
vision of a world set free from sin and affliction;
however, he is a realist. He knows the rejection a
prophet faces. Jesus returns to Cana where he had
changed water to wine (Jn 2:1–11). John calls such
miracles "signs," evidence that a new order has come

about through Jesus. In Cana, a royal official approaches Jesus and begs him to heal his dying son. Jesus is dismayed because the people refuse to believe in him unless they witness signs and wonders. Jesus invites the man to have faith in who he is. When the official persists in pleading for his son's life, Jesus tells him to return to his home as his son will live. Trusting in Jesus' word, the official sets out. On the way, he is met by his servants who tell him that his son has recovered at the very hour Jesus declared he would live. Because of this "sign," the court official and his household come to believe in Jesus' saving power.

To Consider

- Do I need signs and wonders in order to believe?
- Am I able to persist in believing even when I see no evidence that my prayers are heard?

To Pray

Lord Jesus, help me to have faith in your saving presence. Help me to trust and obey your word.

Tuesday of Fourth Week of Lent

Jn 5:1–3,5–16
    Ezek 47:1–9,12; Ps 46

Stand up, take your mat and walk. — Jn 5:8

To Note

There were three temples built to worship God in
Jerusalem. The first "House of Yahweh" was built
by Solomon about 960 BCE[*] and was destroyed in
587 BCE. The second was built by Zerubbable after
the Babylonian exile. This temple was rebuilt by
Herod the Great and was in existence in Christ's
time. When it was destroyed by the Romans in 70
CE, Christians realized that the Body of Christ, the
church, is the spiritual temple on earth.

To Understand

The prophet Ezekiel has a vision of a wonderful
stream flowing out from the temple. As the prophet
wades into the water, it rises to his ankles, his knees,
and then his waist. It finally becomes a great river
that can only be crossed by swimming. For the
prophet, the temple is the source of God's life-giving

---

[*] *"BCE" is an abbreviation for "Before the Common Era," a
term that corresponds to "BC," "Before Christ." "BCE" is a
religiously neutral term that respects Jews and other non-Christians.*

presence. The psalmist proclaims, "There is a stream whose runlets gladden the city of God." While Jesus is in the holy city of Jerusalem on the sabbath, he stops at a pool in Bethesda. There he sees the blind, lame, disabled, and sick who believed that the first person to get into the pool would be cured when the water became turbulent. Jesus asks a man who had been crippled for thirty-eight years if he wants to be healed. The man answers that no one ever helped him get into the water (a baptismal symbol). Did the man subconsciously blame others for his illness? Did he refuse to take responsibility for his own health? Jesus cures the man by a powerful word, and once again, this "sign" of God's presence in Jesus is surrounded by disbelief. Later, Jesus encounters the man in the temple. Jesus warns him that spiritual sickness is a paralysis that prevents a person from responding to God's grace.

To Consider

- Have I given up on God's power to heal me?
- How would I respond to Jesus' question, "Do you want to be healed?"
- In what ways do I need to "stand up and walk"?

To Pray

Lord Jesus, help me to turn to you in my distress. Heal me so I might be a temple of your loving presence.

Wednesday of Fourth Week of Lent

Jn 5:17–30
    Isa 49:8–15; Ps 145

> *For the Father loves the Son and shows him all that he himself is doing.* — *Jn 5:20*

To Note

Human language is insufficient to describe God. Nor can we reduce God to a particular mode of human experience. When we name God with only masculine images—Lord, King, Father—we limit our understanding of who God is. God is neither male or female but a divine being who transcends all definitions.

To Understand

Israel felt forsaken in the Babylonian captivity. It seemed as if God had abandoned her. Isaiah offers a comforting maternal image of God's love. "Can a mother forget the child of her womb? Neither can God forget you!" The psalmist renders a litany of God's feminine attributes: God is gracious, merciful, kind, compassionate. Jesus shows us the masculine side of God, who is Father. In Jesus' day, a son learned his trade by watching his father at work. Similarly, Jesus imitates his heavenly Father's creative and redemptive work in all that he says and does. When Jesus is accused of violating the sabbath law by healing a cripple (Jn 5:1–16), he declares that God's activity is never-ending. Jesus does not act on his own volition; he does what the Father permits. The Father assigns Jesus the power to exercise judgment and authority over life and death. Jesus grants life to those who believe and condemnation to those who do not. The hour will come when even the dead shall hear his voice. Those who are already dead to sin shall live no more. Whoever has heard and obeyed the Son, and who has believed in the Father who sent him, will be raised to eternal life.

To Consider

- Which image of God has the most meaning for me? Shepherd, Savior, Mother, Father, Judge?
- How does my understanding of God need to be expanded?

To Pray

Lord Jesus, reveal your Father's love to me. Teach me about God as Comforter, Life-giver, Mother.

Thursday of Fourth Week of Lent

Jn 5:31–47
Ex 32:7–14; Ps 106

The very works that I am doing testify on my behalf that the Father has sent me. — Jn 5:36

To Note

The Vatican II Dogmatic Constitution on Divine Revelation is called *Dei Verbum*, the Word of God. The Council sets forth the doctrine on the transmission of divine revelation so that the whole world can "hear the summons to salvation, so that through hearing it may believe, through belief it may hope, through hope it may come to love" (#1).

To Understand

God was really angry. The people seemed to have gone mad; they had made for themselves a golden calf to worship. God's self-revelation was beyond anything that the human hand could fashion: fire, wind, storm, and word. God pointed out a way that was right, but the people went their own depraved way. God's wrath was set ablaze. If they did not understand the significance of fire, they would be consumed by it. Moses, the people's intercessor, stood in the breach, pleading for God to remember the divine promises to Abraham, Isaac, and Israel. The psalmist begs God to "remember the love you bear your people." Jesus came into the world to reveal God's love. Although the people had never seen God, they heard God's voice and saw God at work in the words and deeds of the Son. Jesus speaks of those who testify to this truth. John the Baptist was a lamp set aflame to witness to the light that Jesus came to reveal (Jn 1:7,8:12). The scriptures testify to God's revelation in Jesus. Though the people search God's word to find life, they refuse to come to the one who is God's life-giving word. Now Moses will become their accuser. The great law-giver heard God announce that a prophet would be raised up to whom they must listen (Deut 18:15). Jesus is God's revelation, but the people refuse to believe.

To Consider

- Do I read the scriptures as the printed word or the word of life?
- Do I give witness to Jesus by what I say and do?

To Pray

Lord Jesus, I thank you for revealing God's love to me. Help me to recognize you in the many ways you reveal yourself to me.

Friday of Fourth Week of Lent

Jn 7:1–2,10,25–30
    Wis 2:1,12–22; Ps 34

I have not come on my own. But the one who sent me is true, and you do not know him. — Jn 7:28

To Note

The Feast of Tabernacles or "Booths" (Hebrew *Sukkot*) celebrated the "ingathering" of the harvest and the beginning of the new year. During the festival, the people dwelt in branched huts as a reminder of their desert journey in the exodus. At the beginning of the feast, the temple was illuminated by torches. On the last day, water was poured out on the altar of sacrifice. These symbols recall Jesus, the light of the world, the living water, and our Paschal sacrifice (Jn 4:10, 8:12).

To Understand

The book of Wisdom was written less than a hundred years before the time of Christ. In his writings, the sage emphasizes the divine wisdom found in salvation history. The author writes at a time when he and his companions are suffering oppression at the hands of non-believers. Their enemies utter reproaches against those who follow the way of the Lord. They intend to test the just one who boasts that God is his Father to see whether God will defend him and deliver him from his foes. The psalmist echoes these thoughts: "Many are the troubles of the just man, but out of them all the Lord delivers him." One can see the passion of Jesus Christ exemplified in these verses. Jesus is aware that there are those who are plotting to kill him. When the feast of Tabernacles draws near, some of Jesus' unbelieving relatives urge him to go to Jerusalem to publicly perform his miracles. Jesus chooses to go, but in secret. He will not make a display of God's works. Toward the end of the feast, Jesus teaches in the temple. To those who question his authority, he proclaims aloud that he has not come on his own, but has been sent by one who is true. When they try to arrest him, they are unable to do so because the hour of Jesus passion has not yet come.

To Consider

- Am I able to witness to my faith regardless of my fear of rejection?
- Do I pray for missionaries who are oppressed and persecuted?

To Pray

Lord Jesus, help me to hear your life-giving message. Help me to be fearless in proclaiming your words of truth.

Saturday of Fourth Week of Lent

Jn 7:40–53
   Jer 11:18–20*; Ps 7

Search and you will see that no prophet is to arise from Galilee. — Jn 7:52

To Note

The word "Messiah" (Hebrew Mashiah), meaning "the anointed one," is a term applied to kings and priests. Israel expected the Messiah to come from David's royal house which would "stand firm forever" (2 Sam 7:9–16). Jesus, the Son of David, fulfills this hope but in a different way. He is the suffering servant who is led like a lamb to the slaughter (Isa 53:7), and the Good Shepherd who lays down his life for his people (Jn 10:11).

To Understand

"O searcher of heart and soul, O just God," the psalmist acclaims. God searched David's soul and found him worthy to be the anointed one. David, the shepherd-king, was God's heart's desire (1 Sam 13:14, 16:13). Jeremiah was as innocent of heart as a lamb led to the slaughter. Though the people had set their hearts against him, Jeremiah willingly suf-

---

* *In the* New American Bible, *Jer 11:19–23 is transposed with 12:1-6.*

fered in order to speak God's word. Jesus also suffers for proclaiming God's message. Many doubted that he could be the Messiah of God. The Messiah was to come from David's ancestral home in Bethlehem (Mic 5:1–3). Jesus came from Galilee, the rustic land of the Gentiles to the north which was disdained by the people in Judea. They were looking for a warrior-king who would lead them out of oppression. Jesus was meek and humble of heart. The religious leaders have it in their hearts to arrest Jesus, but the temple guards are impressed by his words and they refuse to bring him in. Nicodemus is one of their number, but he is sincere of heart. He reminds his fellow legal experts of the law's requirement of a fair hearing. But they taunt him saying, "Search the scriptures!" No prophet ever came from such an ignoble place as Galilee.

To Consider

- Do I defend the truth or remain silent for fear of ridicule?
- Do I listen to the voices of today's prophets?

To Pray

Lord Jesus, search my heart and find me worthy. Help me to listen to your voice in the scriptures.

Fifth Sunday of Lent (ABC)

(A) Jn 11:1–45
    Ezek 37:12–14; Ps 130; Rom 8:8–11
(B) Jn 12:20–33
    Jer 31:31–34; Ps 51; Heb 5:7–9
(C) Jn 8:1–11
    Isa 43:16–21; Ps 126; Phil 3:8–14

I am the resurrection and the life. Those who believe in me, even though they die will live. — Jn 11:25

To Note

The last of three scrutinies is celebrated with the elect on the fifth Sunday in Lent in preparation for baptism. Today's scrutiny is meant to uncover and heal anything in the hearts of the elect that keeps them bound, and to strengthen all that is life-giving. We are encouraged to examine our own faults, which prevent us from receiving fullness of life.

To Understand

Dry bones that come to life are an image of our spiritual revival when God breathes life into us. The covenant had been carved on stone when God led the people forth from slavery in Egypt, but the people's hearts were like stone in their response. "Create a new heart in me," the psalmist laments. Jeremiah tells us that days are coming when God will make a new covenant, etched in the hearts of men

66

and women of faith. Isaiah assures us that God will provide a new exodus that will surpass the old. Animated by God's spirit, we will arise like a vast army and march into freedom.

Jesus meets a woman who had lost hope in the future. Caught in the act of adultery, she faces a horrible death by stoning. Although everyone accused her of sin, Jesus asks them to look in their own hearts and examine their motives. One by one, they drop their stones and depart. Jesus does not condone her offense, but he will not condemn her either. He sets her free from sin and gives her a future full of hope. To all who are downcast and burdened, Jesus makes an astonishing announcement: "I am the resurrection and the life." In the face of his own death, Jesus raises Lazarus to new life, a symbol of Christ's resurrection and the hope of our rising to new life in baptism.

To Consider

• Do I condemn others while refusing to look at my own offenses?

• What is the "stone" of judgment that I need to let go of today?

To Pray

Lord Jesus, remove all the constraints that keep me from loving others as you do. Raise me to new life with you.

Monday of Fifth Week of Lent

Jn 8:1–11 or Jn 8:12–20 (when Year C is used on Sunday)
  Dan 13:1–9,15–17,19–30,33–62; Ps 23

*Let anyone among you who is without sin be the first to
throw a stone at her.* — Jn 8:7

To Note

The presentation of the Lord's prayer to the elect
takes place during the week following the third scrutiny (Fifth Sunday). The prayer Jesus taught to his
disciples is the whole story of salvation from sin to
grace. God's people pray that they will be delivered
from evil and fed at the eternal banquet so they can
live in God's kingdom and worship the Father on
earth and in heaven.

To Understand

Susanna, a beautiful woman trained in the law of
Moses, is in a dilemma. Two elders, appointed as
judges over Israel, have set a trap to seduce her. If
she does not give in to their lust, they will accuse her
of having an affair with a young man. Susanna knows
she cannot escape their power, but if she consents,
then morally she is as good as dead. Susanna puts her
trust in God and cries for help. The judges accuse
her, and she is condemned to die. As she is led to her
death, the young hero Daniel comes to her aid. When
he discovers a contradiction in the judges' stories, the

death penalty proposed for the woman is inflicted on them. The shepherd-psalmist praises God for giving him courage when beset by darkness and evil. He is confident in God's mercy all the days of his life. Jesus is placed in a dilemma when the legal experts bring a woman to him charged with the sin of adultery. The law of Moses prescribed death (Lev 20:10), but Roman law prohibited their taking life. As judge of life and death, Jesus reads the verdict. Only those without sin should raise their hands against the woman. When her accusers slink away, Jesus tells the woman that he has not come to judge her but to save her. Jesus is the light of the world. His followers need not fear the darkness because they possess the light of life.

To Consider

- Do I put my trust in God when I am confronted by evil?
- Do I have faith in God's love or fear God as judge?
- Am I willing to come to Christ when I have sinned?

To Pray

Lord Jesus, deliver me from temptation and guard me from evil. Lead me to your kingdom where I may dwell with you and your Father forever.

Tuesday of Fifth Week of Lent

Jn 8:21–30
   Num 21:4–9; Ps 102

*When you have lifted up the Son of Man, then you will
realize that I am he. — Jn 8:28*

To Note

The cross is the sign of all who believe in the mystery
of Christ's saving death. The cross is folly to non-believers, but to those who believe, it expresses the
wisdom of God's plan (1 Cor 1:18–21). Christ crucified is the summation of Paul's preaching (1 Cor 2:2).
The cross is a sign of our deliverance from sin and
our reconciliation with God. It is a symbol of suffering and death freely accepted by Christ and his
followers (Mt 16:24).

To Understand

As the people journey through the wilderness to the
promised land, they forget that they have been delivered from evil. Hungry, tired and disgusted, they
complain against God and Moses. In punishment,
they are bitten by deadly serpents. When the people
repent, Moses is instructed to make a symbolic serpent and mount it on a staff. When the people look
at the serpent, it will be a sign of God's power over
evil in the garden of Eden (Gen 3:14), and they will
be healed. The psalmist acclaims God's kindness.

All generations to come will praise God for having heard the cry of those in distress. Jesus comes to reveal God's mercy to a world held captive by evil, a grip that cannot hold him. Set free by his death and resurrection, Jesus will return to the one above who sent him. Jesus warns the self-righteous people that they belong to the world below. They will all die in their sins if they do not repent. When Jesus is lifted up, exalted on the cross, they will realize who he is. Like the bronze serpent, the cross is at once a symbol of life and death, sin and grace, pain and healing. Jesus uses the divine name revealed to Moses, "I AM" (Ex 3:14), to refer to himself. Jesus and the Father are one. God will never abandon him, even in his agony on the cross.

To Consider

- What is my understanding of the cross?
- Do I appreciate its power to save me?
- Does the cross give me confidence in the resurrection?

To Pray

Lord Jesus, as I gaze upon your cross, I pray for healing and life for all those afflicted. Deliver us from evil.

Wednesday of Fifth Week of Lent

Jn 8:31–42
Dan 3:14–20, 91–92,95; Psalm: Dan 3

So if the son makes you free, you will be free indeed.
— Jn 8:36

To Note

The Hebrew word for truth, *emet* is not intellectual belief, but something demanding personal commitment. It is comparable to the *amen* ("so be it") that expresses the steadfastness and reliably to which one gives assent. As the perfect revelation of God, Jesus is the truth (Jn 14:6). The spirit reveals all truth (Jn 16:13) and sets us free to live the truth (Jn 8:32). Our words and deeds are true when we live in fidelity to the truth Christ has revealed.

To Understand

Even the threat of a fiery furnace did not make Shadrach, Meshach, and Abednego worship the golden statue King Nebuchadnezzar had erected. The youths knew the one true God of Israel and not even death would dissuade them from proclaiming the truth. "If God wants to save us, we will be saved. If God chooses not to save us, we still will not worship an idol!" When the boys were cast into the white-hot furnace, Nebuchadnezzar was amazed. "Didn't we throw three youths into the fire? How is it I see four walking unharmed, and the fourth resembles a son of God?" God delivered the faithful servants who refused to worship any god but their own. Jesus comes to reveal God's truth that liberates us from oppression. Those who were listening to Jesus' words take offense. As descendants of Abraham, they claim that they have never been subject to anyone. Jesus says that they are prisoners of sin and he can set them free. To be true children of Abraham, they must follow his example of complete faith and trust in God. By their refusal to believe, they show that they are not children of God's faithful one. Jesus knows they are plotting to kill him, but fear of death will not prevent him from revealing the truth.

To Consider

• Do my words and actions liberate others or hold them in bondage?
• In what ways am I unfree?
• How can I work for the liberation of all peoples?

To Pray

Lord Jesus, I praise you for helping us to live as free sons and daughters of God.

Thursday of Fifth Week of Lent

Jn 8:51–59
    Gen 17:3–9; Ps 105

Very truly, I tell you, before Abraham was, I am.
— Jn 8:58

To Note

Yahweh, God's personal name revealed to Moses (Ex 3:13–15), has been interpreted as "I am who I am" or "the one who causes all things to be." *Yahweh* was written *YHWH* because ancient writing was composed without vowels. When the Jews stopped pronouncing the sacred name out of respect, the word *Adonai* (Hebrew *Lord*) was used in its place. A hybrid combination of the vowels and consonants of these words created the inaccurate *YaHoWaH*, or "Jehovah."

To Understand

Abraham and Sarah were "as good as dead" (Rom 4:19). Without heirs in the society of that day, there was no hope in the future. Then God made an exorbitant promise to Abraham. God would render him exceedingly fertile. Nations and kings would stem from him! As an everlasting pact, the promised land would be their permanent possession. This promise was not just for Abraham, but for all of his offspring. The psalmist reminds us that we are Abraham's descendants. God is faithful and will not forget the covenant made with Abraham. Jesus makes some pretty astonishing promises too. Whoever is true to his word will never see death, a pledge of eternal life for God's chosen ones. The people protest: "Abraham is dead! So are all the prophets! Do you think you are greater than them?" Jesus says that Abraham eagerly anticipated the day when the divine promises would be fulfilled in him. The people retort: "Abraham has been dead for hundreds of years. You're not even fifty!" Jesus makes another outrageous claim: "Before Abraham was, I AM!" His statement implies his preexistence with God (Jn 1:1–3). The unbelievers try to stone him for this blasphemy, but for the time-being, Jesus evades their attempt to kill him.

To Consider

- What are my beliefs about eternal life?
- Could I explain this to someone else?
- How have I experienced God's faithfulness?

To Pray

Lord God, help me to trust in your promises and live with confidence in eternal life.

Friday of Fifth Week of Lent

Jn 10:31–42
   Jer 20:10–13; Ps 18

*Believe the works, so that you may know and
understand that the Father is in me and I in the Father.*
— *Jn 10:38*

To Note

Is faith and works an either/or condition for salvation? The verdict of the Reformation was *sola fides* or
justification by God's grace alone, not by works. This
question was raised in the Christian Scriptures. Paul
says that we are justified through faith (Rom 3:21–
22); nevertheless, James says that God works in the
hearts of believers to produce good fruits. The deeds
of a Christian give evidence of a life of faith (Jas
2:14–17).

To Understand

Jeremiah had a tough time being God's spokesman.
He heard the whispered plans of those who would
betray him. He was aware of the traps his enemies
were setting for him. Sometimes he even felt as if
God had tricked him (Jer 20:7). It was a moment of
crisis for the prophet as he struggled to preserve his
life and his faith at the same time. Yet in the midst
of contradictions, Jeremiah still believed that God
was with him. The psalmist recites a litany as he cries

to God for protection. God is his rock, fortress, deliverer, refuge, shield, horn of salvation, and a stronghold against his enemies. Jesus faces his enemies who are trying to stone him. They had heard his words and seen his deeds, yet they accuse him of making himself out to be God. Jesus tells them that scripture calls the judges in Israel's assembly "gods" and "sons of the Most High" because God's word was transmitted through them (Ps 82:6). How then do they claim that he blasphemed? Jesus says that if they cannot put faith in what he tells them, then at least they can see God acting in the works that he does. While some try to arrest him for speaking the truth, others come to believe in him.

To Consider

- Do I face opposition with confidence in the Lord's presence?
- Do I give witness only by my words or do my deeds also testify to my faith?

To Pray

Lord God, you are my strength and my refuge in times of trouble. Help me to turn to you in adversity.

Saturday of Fifth Week of Lent

Jn 11:45–57
  Ezek 37:21–28; Psalm: Jer 31

*It is better for you to have one man die for the people
than to have the whole nation destroyed. — Jn 11:50*

To Note

The city of Jerusalem suffered a number of invasions
by Rome. In 63 BCE Pompey stormed the city, and
in the year 70 CE Vespasian and Titus virtually
destroyed Jerusalem and the temple. This was the
end of Jerusalem as a Jewish center until modern
times. Jerusalem became a theological symbol of
God's presence in the messianic kingdom, and a
source of revelation to the whole world (Isa 60).

To Understand

The nation of Israel had been divided and con-
quered, some taken captive by Assyria, some by the
Babylonians. The prophet Ezekiel promises restoration. The people will be gathered from all the places
they have been scattered and brought back to their
land. When the people learn to live by the divine
decrees, all nations will know that it is God who
makes them holy. The prophet Jeremiah says that
God will turn their mourning into joy when they
return from all the distant nations. Caiaphas, the high
priest in Jesus' day, unwittingly declares that Jesus

78

would die for the sake of the nation. The religious leaders are afraid that the works that Jesus does will incite the people. If word gets back to Rome, the wrath of the empire will be brought down on their heads and their nation will perish. It is ironic that the great miracle of raising Lazarus to life (Jn 11:43–44) has led to their determination to put Jesus to death. As the feast of Passover draws near, the great celebration of the liberation of God's people, they wonder if Jesus will come to the feast. They begin to be on the lookout for him in order to apprehend him. Jesus, the master of his own destiny, withdraws to a region near the desert where he continues to teach the people.

To Consider

- Am I aware that God's plan is never obstructed by evil forces?
- Have I seen good come from disaster?
- Can I trust this for my own life?

To Pray

Lord God, I pray that the nations will gather one day to give you praise. Deliver all your people from destruction.

Passion (Palm) Sunday (ABC)

(A) Mt 26:14–27:66
    (ABC) Isa 50:4–7; Ps 22; Phil 2:6–11
(B) Mk 14:1–15:47
(C) Lk 22:14–23:56

Father, if you are willing, take this cup away from me;
still, not my will but yours be done. — Lk 22:42

To Note

The procession with palms in the liturgy represents
the triumphal entry of Jesus into Jerusalem, when
branches were strewn in his path to honor him. It is
a joyous demonstration of our fidelity to Christ. The
palms are blessed and distributed to the faithful as
sacramentals. The burning of the palms on the following Ash Wednesday is a symbol of Christ's passion and death and of our own mortality.

To Understand

Paul tells the Christian community that they need an
attitude adjustment. Instead of becoming self-cen-
tered and looking after their own interests, they must
become like Christ, who became a humble servant.
When Jesus' disciples argue over which of them is
the greatest, he tells them that those with worldly
authority lord it over others. If his disciples aspire to
true greatness, they must be willing to become servants of all. At the table, Jesus demonstrates this by

being the one who serves. In the bread and wine of the sacred meal, Jesus inaugurates a new covenant by giving his body and blood for all. Not everyone at the table learned this lesson of love; Jesus is betrayed by one of his own. In the garden of Gethsemane, Jesus empties himself of glory and obediently accepts the bitter cup of suffering. In the garden of Eden, Adam was disobedient, grasping at power as he tried to achieve equality with God. Jesus humbly submits himself to God's will. In his agony on the cross, Jesus prays Psalm 22, "My God, my God, why have you forsaken me?" Yet in the end, God does not abandon him. Jesus is triumphantly raised to new life. As Jesus seals the new covenant with his blood, a Gentile soldier acclaims that truly this is God's own son. Jesus is God's suffering servant, who dies so that all may live.

To Consider

• Do I see myself in those who participated in the crucifixion of Jesus? In the Sanhedrin? Judas? Pilate? the crowd? Do I see myself in those who were faithful to Jesus?

To Pray

Lord Jesus, help me to imitate your faithfulness and serve others even when I have been mocked and betrayed.

Monday of Holy Week

Jn 12:1–11
  Isa 42:1–7; Ps 27

*You always have the poor with you, but you do not
always have me. — Jn 12:8*

To Note

In the Book of Isaiah, scholars have identified four
oracles that describe a mysterious servant of the Lord
(Isa 42:1–4; 49:1–7; 50:4–11; 52:13–53:12). The servant suffered in order to bring sinful people back to
the Lord. It is not certain who the author had in
mind—the prophet himself, a king, the nation of
Israel, the Messiah to come—but the church sees
Jesus Christ as the fulfillment of God's suffering
servant.

To Understand

The first suffering servant oracle announces the purpose for God's servant: to bring forth justice to the
nations. The servant will not have to shout out his
message; his actions will speak louder than his words.
He will proclaim justice by showing mercy to the
poor and helpless, and by liberating all those held
captive in the darkness of their pain. Jesus is God's
servant who suffers for the sake of the people. He is
the anointed one, the Messiah of God, chosen to
proclaim the message of salvation to those who await

his teaching. Jesus demonstrates this when he raises Lazarus from the dead, an act which leads to Jesus' own death (Jn 11:53). When Jesus is honored at a meal in Bethany, Martha characteristically serves while her sister Mary kneels at his feet (Lk 10:38–39). Mary pours out her love for Jesus by anointing his feet, an act suggesting the burial rite. Judas sees this as an extravagant waste, and protests that the money could be better used for the poor. Jesus knows that the real motive is greed, as Judas has been secretly pilfering the donations. Jesus affirms that the woman's deed has not been wasted. Just as her ointment filled the house with the fragrance of her kindness, Jesus' teaching will be an unction for the whole world.

To Consider

- How have I used my gifts to glorify God and serve others this Lent?
- What act of kindness can I show someone today?

To Pray

Lord Jesus, I want my life to be a sweet aroma of your love. Help me to show devotion to you by my concern for others.

Tuesday of Holy Week

Jn 13:21–33,36–38
    Isa 49:1–6; Ps 71

Amen, amen, I say to you, one of you will betray me. —
Jn 13:21

To Note

A prophet is not a fortune-teller, but one who speaks
forth God's words. The prophet speaks God's message no matter how difficult the situation. The
prophet often suffers rejection and persecution from
those who refuse to hear the message. The prophet
warns the people of the consequences of their sins,
but also gives them hope in God's willingness to save
them.

To Understand

In this second of four oracles in the Book of Isaiah,
the Servant of the Lord is God's voice to the world:
"Hear me, O coastlands! Listen, O distant peoples."
In their captivity in Babylon, it seemed as if Israel
was back in Egypt, but Isaiah announces a new
exodus. Though at times God's servant felt that he
toiled in vain, his words are like a sharp-edged sword
that cuts through the darkness and reveals God's
light. Jesus Christ is more than a prophet who speaks
God's words. He is God's word who gives light to the
nations (Jn 1:1–5). Like the Servant of the Lord,

Jesus suffers loss and betrayal for proclaiming God's message. At the Passover feast, Jesus makes the solemn declaration that one of his own disciples will betray him, one with whom he shares a morsel (probably the bitter herbs dipped in salt water, a symbol of the tears shed in slavery). Judas takes the morsel from Jesus' hand, then rushes into the night to accomplish his dark deed. Although Peter is confused by the events, he bravely declares that he will follow Jesus wherever he goes and willingly lay down his life for him. Jesus tells Peter that he too will betray him. As the struggle between light and darkness intensifies, Jesus knows that he must make this final journey alone.

To Consider

- Do I feel that the role of a servant is too degrading?
- How is God glorified through acts of service to others?
- Whom can I serve today?

To Pray

Lord Jesus, help me to forgive those who have betrayed me. Help me to follow your example of love and forgiveness when the going is hard.

Wednesday of Holy Week

Mt 26:14–25
   Isa 50:4–9; Ps 69

Woe to that one by whom the Son of Man is betrayed!
— Mt 26:24

To Note

In his death on the cross, Christ made reparation for
the sins of humankind. Reparation is one of the
conditions of penance. This may entail repairing our
relationship with God, making amends for the dam-
age done to a person's reputation, or recompense for
losses sustained through an immoral action. An act of
reparation is a conscious turning to God for mercy
leading to reconciliation with others.

To Understand

In the third of four Suffering Servant oracles, Isaiah
responds to the people's complaint that they have
been abandoned by God. The prophet knows that
God is near to them even though they have been
banished in exile. Isaiah can speak God's message of
comfort because he first has listened. He willingly
suffers mistreatment in order to proclaim God's word
of salvation. Judas Iscariot, one of Jesus' own disciples, does not recognize Jesus as the source of salvation. Judas hatches a plot with the chief priests to
betray Jesus for the petty sum of thirty pieces of

silver, the price given in compensation for a wounded slave (Ex 21:32). Did ambition for political power cloud Judas' mind when he saw the cross close at hand? Had he closed his ears to Jesus' words that he was God's suffering servant? Did Judas fail to understand the consequences of his betrayal? Was he lying to himself about his own culpability? "Surely it is not I, Rabbi?" The enormity of Judas' sin is brought out by the fact that he openly shares a meal with Jesus while secretly plotting against him. Though Judas' actions fulfill Jesus' words that he would be handed over to his accusers, Judas is responsible for his own misguided deed.

To Consider

- Do I face my sins or try to hide from them?
- Am I humble enough to admit when I am wrong?
- Does pride keep me from being reconciled with someone I have offended?

To Pray

Lord Jesus, I pray for all those who do not listen to your voice, who cannot listen and who will not listen.

Holy Thursday:
Mass of the Lord's Supper

Jn 13:1–15
   Ex 12:1–8,11–14; Ps 116; 1 Cor 11:23–26

*For I have set you an example, that you also should do
as I have done to you. — Jn 13:15*

To Note

Holy Thursday commemorates the institution of the
Eucharist and opens the Easter Triduum (Holy
Thursday, Good Friday and Holy Saturday), three
days of prayer in preparation for Easter, the most
exalted feast of the year. Holy Thursday (also called
Maundy Thursday) centers on Christ's mandatum to
love one another illustrated by his self-gift in the
washing of the feet and the Lord's Supper.

To Understand

The Passover (Hebrew *pesach*) meal was held in
preparation for Israel's march to freedom when the
final plague would "pass over" their houses. This
annual feast is a memorial making the liberation from
slavery present to all generations. The meal begins
with the host blessing a cup of wine. Then bitter
herbs are eaten as a reminder of the Jews' suffering
in Egypt. The host explains the elements of the
rite—wine, unleavened bread, and the flesh of a

sacrificed lamb—and then a second cup of wine is drunk. Then the bread is blessed, broken and distributed, the lamb is shared, and a third cup of wine is drunk. It is this last ritual that Jesus transforms into the perpetual memorial which is our Christian Eucharist. In John's gospel, the only eucharistic action is the washing of the feet. Jesus' command to "do this in memory of me" is demonstrated by an example for his disciples to follow. On the threshold of his passion, Jesus, the servant of the Lord, reveals himself as the servant of all. When Peter objects to Jesus' debasing himself, Jesus insists that being washed (a baptismal symbol) is essential to membership in his body. Jesus shows his disciples that to give love, they must first be able to receive love. The eucharistic celebration makes Christ's saving death on the cross present to all who share the sacred meal.

To Consider

- Do I understand Christ's command to "do this in memory of me" not only as a mandate to break the bread and drink the wine but also as a mandate to love and serve one another?
- Whose feet do I need to wash today?

To Pray

Lord Jesus, help me to live the sacraments of baptism and Eucharist by following your example of loving service.

Good Friday:
Passion and Death of the Lord

Jn 18:1–19:42
    Isa 52:13–53:12; Ps 31; Heb 4:14–16,5:7–9

It is finished. — Jn 19:30

To Note

The accusation that Jesus incited sedition by claiming to be king was written on a sign and placed above his head at the crucifixion. The inscription, written in the international languages of Hebrew, Latin, and Greek, is often abbreviated "INRI." These are the first letters of the Latin *Iesus Nazarenus Rex Iudaeorum* ("Jesus of Nazareth, King of the Jews"). The sign stood as a testimony of Christ's eternal rule over all peoples.

To Understand

"Who would believe what we have heard?" the prophet Isaiah asks in his fourth and final Servant of the Lord oracles. Nations and kings stand speechless before the mystery of redemptive suffering. Israel believed that suffering was just punishment for sin, but the prophet breaks with that tradition. The servant had done no wrong, yet he is condemned to death. Like a sacrificial lamb led to the slaughter, the servant gives his life as an offering for sin. The Song of the Suffering Servant is a prelude to the work of Christ's redemption of humankind. Though innocent, Jesus is counted among the wicked and condemned to death. He is pierced for our offenses and bears the chastisement that makes us whole. The author of Hebrews sees Jesus as a compassionate high priest who can sympathize with our weaknesses because he has been tested in every way. Therefore, we can confidently approach the throne of grace where we will find mercy and help in time of need. John sees Jesus as the master of his own destiny. Jesus appears before Pilate's judgment seat, not as the accused, but as the true judge of the world. Because he surrendered himself to death, he shall take away the sins of many. On the cross, Jesus serenely finishes the work God gave him, then hands over the Spirit to the world he had come to save.

To Consider

• Meditate on a crucifix with the words "Behold your king." How can you offer your life for someone today?

To Pray

Lord Jesus, I venerate your cross, I praise your resurrection. Through your death, you brought life to the world.

Holy Saturday: Easter Vigil (ABC)

(A) Mt 28:1–10

    (ABC) Ex* 14:15–15:1; Ps 118; Rom 6:3–11

(B) Mk 16:1–8

(C) Lk 24:1–12

> *He is not here, but has risen. — Lk 24:5*

To Note

The sacraments of initiation—baptism, confirmation and Eucharist—are the means by which a person enters the faith life of the church. In baptism, the death and resurrection of Christ is accomplished in the dying and rising of his people. In confirmation, the grace of the Spirit enables Christians to carry out their mission in the world. The eucharistic banquet re-presents the new covenant of the Paschal mystery. As an expression of unity, we proclaim our faith by the renewal of our baptismal promises.

To Understand

"Fear not!" Moses told the Israelites as they faced the foe with their backs to the sea. When Israel saw their enemies lying dead on the shore, they beheld

---

* *Nine readings are assigned to the Easter vigil: seven from the Hebrew Scriptures, two from the Christian Scriptures. While the number may be less, the reading from Exodus should always be used.*

the great power of God and believed. With faith, we believe that Christ freed us from the powers of sin and death. Without faith, we are dead to sin and cannot rise to new life. The good news of Christ's resurrection is announced on the "first day of the week," the Christian sabbath. The messenger of the Lord speaks words of encouragement to women who have come to the tomb: "Do not be afraid! Jesus the crucified has been raised just as he said!" While the unbelieving guards lie prostrate with fear, the faith-filled women run to proclaim the good news to Jesus' disciples, though fearful that no one will believe their testimony. Jesus appears to them repeating the angel's message: "Peace! Do not be afraid! Go and carry the news to my brothers." Like the women at the tomb, each of us has a choice to continue looking for fulfillment in the wrong places or to find new life in the risen Lord.

To Consider

- Am I bewildered and fearful about life, or am I confident and hopeful?
- Can I help others find Christ today?

To Pray

Risen Lord, help me to reject sin so that I can live in the freedom of God's children.

Part Two

Easter Sunday to Pentecost Sunday

Easter Sunday:
The Resurrection of the Lord

Jn 20:1–9
> or (A) Mt 28:1–10 or (B) Mk 16:1–8 or (C) Lk 24:1–12
> Acts 10:34,37–43; Ps 118; Col 3:1–4 or 1 Cor 5:6–8

He saw and believed. — Jn 20:8

To Note

Israel came to believe that a just God could not abandon the souls of the righteous to the netherworld (*Sheol*). Around the time of the martyrdom of the Maccabees (second century BCE), they came to a belief in the resurrection (2 Macc 7:9). The church's doctrine of the resurrection is expressed in the proclamation of faith, "Jesus is Lord!" Jesus is the first-born from the dead (Col 1:18), and the first-fruits (1 Cor 15:20) of our own hope in eternal life.

To Understand

He was dead! Now he is alive! This is the incredible good news that Peter proclaims. Peter knows that Christ's new life is not simply the resuscitation of a corpse, but a whole new existence. Peter didn't comprehend this all at once. Mary Magdalene didn't either. She only knew that the Lord's body was no longer in the tomb. When Peter saw the shroud lying in the empty tomb, he failed to grasp its meaning. John was quicker to understand. He observed the same evidence and believed. With the light of the Spirit, the disciples came to an understanding of what it meant to rise from the dead. The author of Colossians reminds us that while we share in Christ's resurrection, we also participate in his death. "You have died!" he says emphatically; but if we keep our focus on what is above rather than below, we will experience his glory. Paul compares the new life we receive in baptism to fresh dough, devoid of leaven that corrupts. He tells us to do away with moral decay and to celebrate the feast with the unleavened bread of sincerity and truth. Jesus, who ate and drank with his disciples, continues to be present in the eucharistic body, the church. The psalmist invites us to rejoice and be glad on this day that the Lord has made. We have much to celebrate; we shall not die but live!

To Consider

- Do I understand what it means to be raised up with Christ?
- How does my life give evidence to my faith?

To Pray

Risen Lord, help me to believe your promise of eternal life. Let me bear witness to this hope by the way I live.

Monday of the Octave of Easter

Mt 28:8–15
   Acts 2:14,22–32; Ps 16

God raised him up, having freed him from death,
because it was impossible for him to be held in its
power. — *Acts 2:24*

To Note

Kerygma is a Greek term meaning proclamation or
preaching on the core message of salvation. The
kerygma contains the essential facts of Jesus, who by
his death and resurrection has become Christ, our
Lord and Savior. The announcement of this good
news precedes detailed religious instruction (catechesis).

To Understand

The tomb was like a prison cell which could not keep
its hold on Jesus. Peter proclaims the good news,
"God freed him from death's bitter pangs and raised
him up!" Peter looks to the scriptures to interpret
Jesus' dying and rising. David, the great king of
Israel, had died and was buried. His tomb was still in
their midst. Yet David was confident that God would
raise up an heir to the throne who would not undergo
corruption. The psalmist sings of David's faith, "You
show me the path to life." Jesus, the Son of David,
is the fulfillment of God's promise. Everything that

happened to Jesus was a part of God's saving plan. The women who come to mourn at Jesus' tomb are unable to see God's design in their suffering. Yet their sadness suddenly turns into joy. Jesus has broken the bonds of death. As they hurry off to share the good news with their brothers, they fear that their message will not be accepted. Jesus appears with consoling words of peace. Even as these women obey Jesus' command to announce what they have seen, the religious leaders and the military work out a strategy to bury the glad tidings. Those who guarded the tomb are to say that the disciples stole Jesus' body while they were sleeping. But the good news could not be suppressed any more than death could hold God's faithful one.

To Consider

• Am I afraid to announce the good news?

• Do others see the resurrection in my life?

To Pray

Risen Lord, give me confidence to proclaim your message of life in the midst of hopelessness and despair.

Tuesday of the Octave of Easter

Jn 20:11–18
Acts 2:36–41; Ps 33

God has made him both Lord and Messiah, this Jesus whom you crucified. — Acts 2:36

To Note

The Vatican II declaration on non-Christian religions states that while the Jewish authorities pressed for the death of Christ, Jews cannot be indiscriminately "charged with the crimes committed during his passion." Remembering our common heritage, the church "deplores all hatreds, persecutions, displays of anti-semitism leveled at any time or from any source against the Jews" (#4).

To Understand

Peter continues his kerygmatic proclamation. Jesus the crucified has been raised up as Lord and Messiah. Those who hear his preaching are moved to ask, "What are we to do, my brother?" Peter's reply: "Repent and be baptized." The promise is made not only to those who heard the message of salvation, but to all those far off who have not yet heard God's call. The psalmist praises God's word as being trustworthy. All who hope in God's mercy will be delivered from death. Mary Magdalene had lost hope as she stood weeping at the tomb of her Lord. Through her tears, Mary peers inside the dark tomb where Jesus' body had lain. Instead of death she now finds two messengers of light. "Woman," they ask, "why are you weeping?" She barely can answer when she hears Jesus ask, "What is it you are looking for?" As she turns around (a symbol of conversion), Mary beholds Jesus, whom she believes to be the gardener. When Jesus speaks her name, Mary, she recognizes him as her dear teacher (Hebrew *Rabboni*). In the garden of the new creation, the light of the risen Christ shines on Mary, a redeemed daughter of the Lord. Jesus tells her not to cling to his earthly memory, but to share her joy with her brothers by announcing the good news, "I have seen the Lord!"

To Consider

* What is it I am looking for?
* Do I look in the tomb of darkness and death or in the garden of light and life?

To Pray

Risen Lord, help me to bring your peace and forgiveness to others. Help me to announce this good news to all I meet.

Wednesday of the Octave of Easter

Lk 24:13–35
   Acts 3:1–10; Ps 105

Was it not necessary that the Messiah should suffer these things and then enter into his glory? — Lk 24:26

To Note

A sacrifice is the giving away or the offering up of something valuable. The ancient sacrifice was usually an animal whose blood was poured out on the altar in recompense to God for the sins of the people. Jesus willingly offered himself as a sacrifice for our sins. In the Eucharist, we give thanksgiving for this loving gift.

To Understand

The temple gate was called Beautiful, but life wasn't beautiful for the lame man who sat there begging for alms each day. Then two of Jesus' disciples came into his life and he received something infinitely more valuable than silver or gold. "In the name of Jesus Christ, walk," Peter said as he grasped the man by the hand and raised him up. To everyone's amazement, the man not only walked, but leaped with joy as he gave thanks to God for the wondrous thing that had happened. Two other disciples discovered that suffering often precedes new life. Although they were not crippled, they were filled with hopelessness. The two were returning from their Passover pilgrimage to Jerusalem, where they had witnessed the tragic events that occurred there. As they walked along the road to Emmaus, a stranger joined them and they shared their disappointment with him, "We had hoped that Jesus would be the one who would set Israel free." Then the stranger explained the scriptures to show that it was necessary for the Messiah to suffer so as to be raised to new life. By nightfall, a spark of hope was enkindled in their hearts and they begged the stranger to stay with them. While at table, the disciples' eyes were opened and they recognized Jesus in the breaking of the bread. Filled with new life, they leaped up and returned to Jerusalem. "The Lord has been raised," they joyfully told Peter, "It is true!"

To Consider

- Is Jesus a stranger on my life's journey?
- Does my heart burn with fervor when I hear the scriptures proclaimed?
- Do I recognize Jesus in the breaking of the bread?

To Pray

Recite your own litany of thanksgiving for the good things you have received from the Lord.

Thursday of the Octave of Easter

Lk 24:35–48
  Acts 3:11–26; Ps 8

*God fulfilled what he had foretold through all the
prophets, that his Messiah would suffer. — Acts 3:18*

To Note

The Hebrew Bible is divided into three categories:
the Law ("Torah"), the Prophets ("Nebiim," subdi-
vided into the "Former" and "Latter" prophets),
and the Writings ("Ketubim"). The Greek translation (Septuagint) is divided into four categories: the
Pentateuch, the Historical books, the Wisdom books
and the Prophets.

To Understand

"Why does this surprise you?" Peter asks the crowds
who are in awe when the lame man is cured. "This
man wasn't raised up by our power," Peter assures
them, "but by faith and trust in Jesus' name."
Though the people acted out of ignorance when
they put Jesus to death, God raised him up in fulfillment of the scriptures. Moses foretold that a new
prophet would be raised up from among them (Deut
18:15). If they would listen to this prophet and repent of their evil ways, God would bless them and
all the families of the world. "O Lord, our Sovereign,

104

how majestic is your name in all the earth!" the psalmist acclaims.

The two disciples from Emmaus also praise the marvelous works of God. They had come to know the risen Christ in the breaking of the bread. Although Jesus had disappeared from their sight, he reappears in their midst. Jesus offers the gift of peace to his startled followers. He reassures them that he is not a ghost by showing them his wounds and sharing a meal with them. He tells them that all the scriptures—the law of Moses, the prophets, and the psalms—anticipated his dying and rising. Jesus' disciples have witnessed these events, and now they must proclaim a message of repentance for the forgiveness of sins to all the nations.

To Consider

- Do I listen to Christ's words in the scriptures?
- Do I act on the word by repenting of my sins?
- Do I proclaim this message of peace and mercy to others?

To Pray

Risen Lord, give me your peace when I am fearful. Forgive me my sins so I can offer forgiveness to others.

Friday of the Octave of Easter

Jn 21:1–14
   Acts 4:1–12; Ps 118

*There is salvation in no one else, for there is no other
name under heaven given among mortals by which we
must be saved. — Acts 4:12*

To Note

The word salvation is an all-inclusive word for being
"made safe" or "rescued" from suffering and evil
through the mighty acts of God. In the Hebrew
Scriptures, humankind was saved from evil by their
deliverance through the waters of the sea. In the
Christian Scriptures, Jesus liberates us from the
bondage of sin and death through the waters of
baptism.

To Understand

"How could such commonplace men like you do
such an amazing thing as cure a cripple?" The incredulous religious leaders interrogate Peter and
John. The Holy Spirit gives Peter the courage to
answer that this good deed wasn't done by any power
of their own. The lame man was healed by the
authority of Jesus Christ, whom they crucified, but
whom God raised from the dead. The name of Jesus
offers salvation for the whole world. Peter felt the
strength of the Spirit, but he also knew what it was

like to be powerless. After Jesus' death on the cross, he wanted to go back to his ordinary life. "I'm going fishing," he told the other disciples, thinking their service was at an end. "We'll go with you," the others were quick to reply. Without Jesus to guide them, their efforts were futile and they caught nothing. At daybreak, the risen Lord appears on the shore and directs them to lower their nets. When they obey his command, they catch so many fish that their nets can hardly hold them. In spite of the great number, the nets are not torn, a symbol of the time when all people would be gathered in unity and faith in Jesus' name. When the disciples recognize Jesus, they come ashore, where they share a meal with him. Through baptism and the Eucharist, the risen Christ empowers his disciples for their mission to the world.

To Consider

- When has the Lord asked me to cast my nets in a different direction?
- What was the result of my efforts?
- Did I feel strengthened by the Lord's presence?

To Pray

Slowly repeat the name of Jesus and reflect on the meaning of salvation in your life.

Saturday of the Octave of Easter

Mk 16:9–15
> Acts 4:13–21; Ps 118

We cannot keep from speaking about what we have seen and heard. — Acts 4:20

To Note

The National Catechetical Directory states: "Faith calls for responses of assent, trust, surrender, and obedience to God. Thus faith means commitment, and in this sense it is a deep personal relationship with the Lord. Moments of doubt and anxiety, arising from our weakness, can be expected in the life of faith" (#57).

To Understand

Uneducated men of no social standing. A cripple. A demon-filled woman. A couple of nobodies. What could these insignificant people know about important religious matters? Yet lives were changed, people were healed, the good news was spread through them. "Let's put a stop to it," the religious people said. "We've never done it that way before! That's not our tradition!" They warned Peter and John never to speak of Jesus or teach about him again. Peter and John stood firm: "Whom shall we obey, you or God? We can't help talking about what we've seen and heard." Peter and John had erred the same way in their refusal to believe the testimony of others, but they had learned from their mistake. When Mary Magdalene had told them the good news that Jesus was alive, they refused to believe her. "What could a woman's testimony be worth?" When the disciples from Emmaus had told them that they had met the risen Lord while walking along the road, they were incredulous. "Why would the Lord appear to them and not us?" Jesus had to take them to task. While they were at table, he revealed himself to them. Even though Jesus rebuked them for their disbelief, he told them, "Go into all the world and proclaim the good news to the whole creation." Even stubborn apostles could be instruments of the risen Christ.

To Consider

- When have I refused to believe the faith experience of others?
- Am I more willing to listen to people of prominence than unimportant people?

To Pray

"Risen Lord, I thank you that you have been my Savior" (Ps 118:21).

Second Sunday of Easter (ABC)

Jn 20:19–31
>   (A) Acts 2:42–47; Ps 118; 1 Pet 1:3–9
>   (B) Acts 4:32–35; Ps 118; 1 Jn 5:1–6
>   (C) Acts 5:12–16; Ps 118; Rev 1:9–11, 12–13,17–19

Yet more than ever believers were added to the Lord,
great numbers of both men and women. — Acts 5:14

To Note

The word "mystagogy" refers to the post-baptismal period of catechesis in the Easter season. The church community and the "neophytes," the newly baptized, share their experience of the sacraments they have received in order to make it a part of their daily lives. It is a time to deepen and strengthen the meaning of the Paschal Mystery for us all.

To Understand

The followers of Jesus may not have understood ecclesiology (the theology of the origin, nature, and mission of the church), but they did understand the need to *be* church. They devoted themselves to the apostles' teaching, had an enthusiastic sense of belonging to the community, faithfully gathered for the eucharistic meal and for prayer, and shared all things in common. How was this possible? Jesus conquers the world and its lust for power and possessions. The love of God enables his followers to love one another.

Jesus demonstrated this love by water and blood. Whether in baptism or crucifixion, this means dying to oneself. The power of love over suffering and evil had a convincing effect on those who witnessed it. More and more people came to believe in the Christ who was present and active in their midst. That sounds great when things are going well, but what about the times of questioning, doubt and crisis? After the crucifixion, it didn't take long for the disciples to waver in their faith. They hid behind the locked doors, shaking in their sandals. Only at the sight of the risen Lord did their faith return. Thomas missed out on this remarkable event and he stubbornly refused to believe the others' testimony without proof. "Peace," Jesus tells doubting Thomas, Peter, John, and us too. "You believe because you see. How blessed are you if you can believe without seeing."

To Consider

- Do my words and actions bear witness to the risen Lord in my life?
- Does my parish give evidence of our faith by serving the needs of the community?

To Pray

Risen Lord, help us to celebrate your resurrection in word and deed so we may enjoy fullness of life with you.

Monday of Second Week of Easter

Jn 3:1–8
   Acts 4:23–31; Ps 2

*No one can enter the kingdom of God without being
born of water and Spirit. — Jn 3:5*

To Note

Catechesis is from the Greek *kat-echeo* meaning to
"echo" or to "resound in the ears," hence to instruct.
Catechesis is the teaching of the doctrine (Greek
didache) of the church based on the life, death and
resurrection of Jesus Christ in preparation for baptism and as a life-long process of learning.

To Understand

Peter and John had been imprisoned for proclaiming
the gospel. The religious leaders warned them to
stop teaching about Jesus, but when they were re-
leased they went right back at it. The Christian
community had been praying for the apostles, and
now they were overjoyed. They raised their voices
in ecstatic praise of God, who had enabled these
servants to speak with courage and to heal in the
name of Jesus. As they prayed, the house where they
were gathered shook with the energy of the Spirit,
and all the people were empowered to speak God's
word with boldness. The psalmist exults in those
who put their trust in the Lord. Though the kings of

the earth conspire against the Lord and his anointed, God's children will overthrow the powerful and rule with an iron rod.

Nicodemus was a man of authority and power in the Jewish Sanhedrin. Because of his prominent office, he came to Jesus at night, a symbol of his need for faith. Nicodemus recognized Jesus as a teacher who came from God as he saw God's power at work in Jesus. Jesus instructs Nicodemus on the necessity of being born of water and Spirit, meaning spiritual rebirth. Jesus says that the workings of the Spirit are invisible. One can only observe its effects in those who are born again through baptism.

To Consider

- Have I recommitted myself to my baptismal promises?
- Have I observed the workings of the Spirit in my life?
- Are others able to see this in me?

To Pray

Risen Lord, teach me to understand my baptismal call to serve my brothers and sisters. Strengthen me to live as God's child.

Tuesday of Second Week of Easter

Jn 3:7–15
 Acts 4:32–37; Ps 93

*If I have told you about earthly things and you do not
believe, how can you believe if I tell you about heavenly
things? — Jn 3:12*

To Note

The Christian Scripture writers struggled to define
the Holy Spirit, whom we know today as the Third
Person of the Trinity. In Greek the word for "wind"
and "spirit" is the same, *pneuma*. The word *pneuma*
is neuter in Greek. The Aramaic word for Spirit, *ruah*
is feminine. The Latin translation *Spiritus* is masculine. To define the Spirit by gender is an inadequate
concept.

To Understand

The members of the early church had a profound
sense of responsibility for one another. Spreading
the good news was hard work and it required the
spiritual and material support of every person. One
such individual was Barnabas, who later became a
companion to Paul on his missionary journeys. The
name "Barnabas" was a nick-name which meant
"son of encouragement," given because he had gen-
erously assisted the apostles in their efforts of evangelization. Although Barnabas had some wealth, he

114

thought more of building up the heavenly reign than he did of amassing earthly possessions. Nicodemus was an influential religious leader who was attracted by Jesus' proclamation of the kingdom. Jesus encourages Nicodemus to seek the things above rather than earthly things. Although Nicodemus holds the office of teacher, Jesus teaches him that entrance into the kingdom depends on spiritual rebirth. Jesus compares the Spirit's action in the life of the believer to the inscrutable movement of the wind. No one can fully understand this mystery without God's grace. Just as Jesus was lifted up on the cross and exalted in his resurrection, Nicodemus must be willing to lay aside his earthly life to achieve life eternal.

To Consider

- What am I doing to build up the reign of God on earth?
- Do I obey the promptings of the Spirit when I must do something difficult?
- Am I more concerned with my position and possessions?

To Pray

Risen Lord, help me to respond with a generous heart to the needs of your people. Help me to be unselfish in my support of those who proclaim the gospel.

Wednesday of Second Week of Easter

Jn 3:16–21
   Acts 5:17–26; Ps 34

*For God so loved the world that he gave his only Son,
so that everyone who believes in him may not perish but
may have eternal life. — Jn 3:16*

To Note

The core of Christian Scripture theology is the love
of God that Jesus came to reveal. By his passion and
death, Jesus reveals the greatest love conceivable.
This is not ordinary human affection but supernatu-
ral love. The love that the Father has for the Son is
the same love that God has for each person. This
indeed is the good news that Jesus shares with the
world.

To Understand

The religious leaders are filled with jealousy over the
success of the apostles who had disobeyed their
order not to mention the name of Jesus in public
again. The twelve are arrested and thrown in jail.
During the night, the prison bars swing open and the
apostles are commanded by God to return to the
temple and continue to teach about their new life in
Christ. The guards are at a loss to explain why their
prisoners are now free. The psalmist sings of his own
liberation, "I sought the Lord, and I was delivered

from all my fears." Jesus teaches Nicodemus about the love of God he came to reveal. God has no desire to condemn the world; God wants to save the world from the destruction of sin. Each individual is given the free will to respond to the grace God offers, or to turn away from it. The choice each person makes determines salvation or condemnation. Rejecting God's love brings self-condemnation. Accepting the love of God sets one free from the chains of darkness and brings one into the freedom of eternal light. Those who practice evil are afraid to come into the light for fear their dark deeds will be exposed. Those who act in truth have no reason to be afraid as their deeds are done in the light of God's grace and love.

To Consider

- Have I made a decision to accept God's love today?
- How will I respond to this love?
- Can love conquer evil in today's world?

To Pray

Risen Lord, illuminate the dark places in my life. Allow your light to shine through me for others.

Thursday of Second Week of Easter

Jn 3:31–36
  Acts 5:27–33; Ps 34

The one who comes from above is above all. — Jn 3:31

To Note

Authority (Greek *exousia*) connotes both the power
and the legal right to give commands and enforce
obedience. Jesus has been lawfully designated by
God with the power to forgive sins. Through the
Holy Spirit, Christians share in Christ's ministry of
reconciliation. To exercise power without authority
is tyrannical. To exercise authority without power is
ineffective.

To Understand

The religious leaders are so furious that they want to
kill the apostles. "We told you never to preach about
that name again!" Did they think by making Jesus
anonymous they could repress the truth? Peter and
the apostles are steadfast. "It is better to obey God's
command than human authority." Even while standing before the Sanhedrin, Peter can't resist preaching. He tells them of Jesus' dying for the forgiveness
of sin, and of his glorious exaltation to rule at God's
side. Peter says that the Spirit of God testifies to the
truth of his words. The psalmist declares, "When the
just cry out, the Lord hears them." God's praise is

ever in his mouth. Jesus teaches with authority. He comes from God and he speaks the words of God. Jesus concludes his discourse to Nicodemus by offering him a choice. Whoever believes in his words will have life eternal. Whoever disobeys him will suffer the wrath of God. We hear nothing of Nicodemus' response. Did he accept or reject the Son? Perhaps he made this decision gradually. Later, Nicodemus courageously demanded that the Sanhedrin give Jesus a fair hearing (Jn 7:50), and he braved the authorities in order to give Jesus a proper burial (19:39). Surely Nicodemus must have accepted Jesus' testimony as the truth.

To Consider

- Do I listen to the full gospel of Jesus, or only those words that I choose to hear?
- Do I speak the truth with love?
- Do I make a daily decision to obey Christ?

To Pray

Risen Lord, help me to listen to your words. Give me courage to bear witness to the truth in all I say and do.

Friday of Second Week of Easter

Jn 6:1–15
   Acts 5:34–42; Ps 27

*Jesus took the loaves, and when he had given thanks, he
distributed them to those who were seated.* — Jn 6:11

To Note

The word "Eucharist" means "to give thanks." The
Eucharist is the sacrifice of praise and thanksgiving
in remembrance of Christ, who as priest and victim
re-presents the covenant effected through his death
and resurrection. The four-fold acts of the Eucharist—to take bread, bless it, give thanks and share
it—represents our deepest unity and our self-offer-
ing in the service of others.

To Understand

Gamaliel was a great teacher of the Pharisees. The
apostle Paul was educated in the law at his feet (Acts
22:3). Gamaliel wisely cautions the Sanhedrin to do
nothing to the apostles. He recalls several agitators
whose followers disbanded on the death of their
leaders. If the Christian movement is of human origin, nothing will come of it. If divine, the Sanhedrin
will be fighting God in their attempt to destroy it. In
spite of Gamaliel's admonition, the Sanhedrin have
the apostles beaten and once again order them not to
speak about Jesus. As the body of Christ, they share

in his sufferings. Instead of being discouraged, the apostles give thanks to God as they boldly continue to proclaim the gospel. The psalmist says, "The Lord is my light and my salvation; whom shall I fear?"

Jesus was moved to pity when he saw the hungry crowds who were following him. Jesus asks his disciples where they can get bread to feed the people, but Philip sees this as an impossible situation. Andrew notices a boy with a few loaves and fish, but cannot see what good that can be with so many to feed. Where they see scarcity, Jesus sees abundance. He takes the simple offering, gives thanks to God, and distributes it to the hungry people. The leftover bread fills twelve baskets, a symbol of the apostolic church which continues to feed God's people in the Eucharist, in the proclamation of the gospel, and in their service to the poor.

To Consider

- Do I see challenges as problems or as opportunities?
- In what ways do I share in the apostolic work of the church?

To Pray

Risen Lord, help me to be your body and blood as I labor for the gospel. Transform my sufferings into joy.

Saturday of Second Week of Easter

Jn 6:16–21
>Acts 6:1–7; Ps 33

>*It is I; do not be afraid. — Jn 6:20*

To Note

Deacons (Greek *diakonos*, "servants") in the early church included men and women who cared for the sick and poor and assisted in baptizing. This office eventually became a step toward ordination for the priesthood. Vatican II restored the permanent diaconate for men and authorized them to preach, instruct, preside over worship and prayer, distribute the Eucharist and to officiate at baptisms, marriages and funerals ("Dogmatic Constitution on the Church," #29).

To Understand

After the death and resurrection of Christ, divisions in the body arose. As the gospel was proclaimed to the Hellenist world, there was an influx of people into the church with differences in language and culture. "Our people aren't getting their share of food," the Greek-speaking disciples complained. "What should we do, neglect preaching the gospel in order to wait on tables?" the apostles argued. Jesus hadn't left a rule book to follow. Guided by the Spirit, the community chose seven wise and spiritual individuals to be servants of the community. The apostles imposed hands on the seven, empowering them for this task. Thus the apostles were free to proclaim the word of God and the church grew in numbers. People are attracted to a community that is an instrument of reconciliation. "The eyes of the Lord are upon those who fear him," the psalmist reminds us. After Jesus' death and resurrection, the church sometimes felt as though the Lord hadn't kept his eyes upon them. When they were tossed about by turmoil and strife, they felt as though he had deserted them. The story of the disciples in the storm at sea tells us that Jesus is present in life's trials. "It is I," he says, "do not be afraid." Though conflict is inevitable, with Jesus in the pilot seat the church is brought to a safe harbor.

To Consider

- How can I be a minister of reconciliation in the midst of dissension?
- Do I pray when decisions must be made?

To Pray

Risen Lord, help me to know you are with me in all the storms of my life. Let me bring your peace when others are fearful.

Third Sunday of Easter (ABC)

(A) Lk 24:13–35
    Acts 2:14,22–28; Ps 16; 1 Pet 1:17–21
(B) Lk 24:35–48
    Acts 3:13–15,17–19; Ps 4; 1 Jn 2:1–5
(C) Jn 21:1–19
    Acts 5:27–32,40–41; Ps 30; Rev 5:11–14

Were not our hearts burning within us while he was talking to us on the road, while he was opening the scriptures to us? — Lk 24:32

To Note

The Dogmatic Constitution on Divine Revelation says that "the church has always venerated the divine scriptures as she venerated the Body of the Lord" and ceaselessly offers it to the faithful from "the one table of the Word of God and the Body of Christ" (#21). The risen Christ is present in the church through word and sacrament.

To Understand

After Jesus had been crucified, the disciples felt as though there was no longer any good news to proclaim. Some of them return to fishing, but even this proves to be unprofitable. Then the risen Christ appears to them and they bring forth a great catch. With Christ in their midst they can do all things. On the shore, Jesus gives Peter three opportunities to be reconciled to him for his three-fold denial. With each declaration of love, Jesus tells Peter to care for his "lambs," the infant Christian community. By following the crucified Lord, Peter will share in his mission, but also in his suffering. Two other disciples are filled with despair as they leave Jerusalem. Although it was resurrection Sunday, for them it was still Good Friday. Suddenly, the risen Christ appears in their midst, but the disciples do not recognize him. As they share their disappointment that Jesus had not set Israel free, the Lord opens their minds to the scriptures. Didn't they understand the Messiah *had* to suffer so as to enter glory? Their eyes are opened when Jesus shares a meal with them. Though Jesus vanishes from their sight, they remember how their hearts burned with joy as he explained the scriptures and how they came to know him in the breaking of the bread.

To Consider

- Do I hear Christ in the proclamation of the word?
- Do I recognize Christ as I break the bread with my brothers and sisters?
- Am I a sign of the Lord's presence?

To Pray

Risen Lord, enkindle a desire in your people for your word and sacrament. Let me speak truth to nourish others.

Monday of Third Week of Easter

Jn 6:22–29
   Acts 6:8–15; Ps 119

You are looking for me, not because you saw signs, but because you ate your fill of the loaves. — Jn 6:26

To Note

The catechism definition of a sacrament is "an outward sign instituted by Christ to give grace." Sacraments are symbolic actions through the Spirit in the church that express God's saving love for us in Christ. Jesus is the "sacrament" of God, the tangible and efficacious sign that communicates God's love. The church is the "sacrament" of Christ, who continues to make his saving presence known in the world through the Holy Spirit.

To Understand

Stephen was one of the first deacons chosen to administer to the Greek-speaking Christians. The signs and wonders he performed gave witness to the power of the risen Christ at work in him. When Stephen's enemies chose to debate with him, they proved no match for his wisdom and spirit. In retaliation, these men persuaded others to charge Stephen of speaking blasphemies against God. They accused him of trying to change the ancient customs Moses handed down to them. Throughout the interrogation, Stephen exhibited the peace that comes from a blameless life. The psalmist affirms: "The way of truth I have chosen. I have set your ordinances before me." Many people who followed Jesus were more impressed by the wonders he performed than they were by his life and teaching. After the miracle of the multiplication of the loaves, they followed him hoping for another manifestation of his power. "You're not looking for me because of who I am, but because you want more bread," Jesus told them bluntly. He knew that it was not perishable food the people needed, but the life-giving food of the Spirit. But they didn't seem to hear him. They asked him how they too could perform the works of God. Jesus told them that the most important work they could do was to believe in the one God had sent to them.

To Consider

- Am I an authentic sign of Christ's presence in the world?
- Do I look for "signs and wonders" or for signs that communicate the wonder of God's love?

To Pray

Risen Lord, help me to seek the way of truth. Let all I do be a sign of your love to the world.

Tuesday of Third Week of Easter

Jn 6:30–35
    Acts 7:51–8:1; Ps 31

*For the bread of God is that which comes down from
heaven and gives life to the world. — Jn 6:33*

To Note

Stephen was the first martyr of the church. The
Greek word *martur* literally meant "witness," one
who testified to the truth in court. With the passage
of time, the church applied the word to those who
bore the ultimate witness to the truth of the gospel
by the sacrifice of their lives in imitation of Jesus
Christ.

To Understand

Stephen may have looked like an angel (Acts 6:15),
but he wasn't afraid to tell it like it was: "you stiff-
necked people, uncircumcised of heart and ears,
opposing the Holy Spirit, persecuting the prophets!"
His indictment went on and on. He knew his time
was short and he wanted to get it all in. When
Stephen looked to the heavens and announced that
he saw Jesus standing at the right hand of God, the
people covered their ears and refused to listen to
him. Then they rushed at him and began stoning
him. Like Jesus, Stephen prayed for God to forgive
those who were killing him. "Into your hands, I

commend my spirit," the psalmist prayed knowing the Lord would redeem him. All during this time, a young man observed everything yet did not understand the meaning of Stephen's death. His name was Saul. One day, the Lord would change his heart and he would become the great evangelist Paul. The crowds who followed Jesus from the wilderness did not truly understand who he was. "What sign can you perform?" they asked. They demanded that he show them a sign from heaven such as the manna that Moses had given their ancestors. They missed the point that Jesus himself was the sign of God's saving love. They were looking for perishable food, while Jesus was food for the "life of the world." No one who comes to him will hunger for anything else.

To Consider

- Do I remain silent when I see injustice because I am afraid of the reactions of others?
- In what ways do I witness to the truth of Jesus' life-giving presence?

To Pray

Risen Lord, fill me with courage to witness to the truth no matter what the consequences. Help me always to hunger and thirst for justice.

Wednesday of Third Week of Easter

Jn 6:35–40
    Acts 8:1–8; Ps 66

I am the bread of life. — *Jn 6:35*

To Note

The Constitution on the Sacred Liturgy states that the liturgy of the word and the eucharistic liturgy, "are so closely connected with each other that they form but one single act of worship" (#56). These two themes are evident in Jesus' discourse on the "bread of life." The first is the "sapiential" or "wisdom" theme (vv 1–50). All who hear Jesus' words hear God's revelation. The second is the "sacramental" theme in which Jesus' body and blood is offered in the bread and wine of the Eucharist.

To Understand

After Stephen's death, persecution broke out in Jerusalem and Christians scattered to safer areas. If this hadn't occurred, would Christianity have remained an isolated phenomena? Because the faithful were dispersed, the word of God spread throughout the world. Among those who persecuted the Christians was Saul, who conducted a malicious house-to-house search for them. Who would have believed that this vengeful man would become Paul, the foremost evangelist of the gospel? Philip, a humble deacon like Stephen, did not restrict his ministry to waiting on tables. Because miracles and healings were worked through him, people paid attention to his preaching of the good news. In this topsy-turvy kingdom, defeat turns into victory, persecutors become proclaimers, and the lowly are exalted. This is surely divine wisdom, not human. Jesus is God's wisdom incarnate. He makes the incredible statement, "I am the bread of life." John sees two aspects to this mystery. All who come to Jesus are nourished by God's truth, which is unchanging and lasts forever. Jesus is the sacrament of God, who satisfies all human longings for unity, peace, reconciliation and eternal life.

To Consider

* Do I hear Jesus' voice when the scriptures are proclaimed?
* Does God's word sustain me daily so that I might bring life to others?

To Pray

Sing or recite praises to Christ's presence in your life (Ps 66:1-5).

Thursday of Third Week of Easter

Jn 6:44–51
   Acts 8:26–40; Ps 66

*No one can come to me unless drawn by the Father who
sent me. — Jn 6:44*

To Note

The sacred synod of Vatican II exhorted all the
Christian faithful to learn "the surpassing knowledge
of Jesus Christ" (Phil 3:8) by frequent reading of the
divine scriptures. 'Ignorance of the scriptures is ignorance of Christ' (St. Jerome)." The synod also
reminded the faithful that "prayer should accompany the reading of sacred scripture" (Divine Revelation #25).

To Understand

Following the Spirit's lead, Philip became a chariot
chaser, an eaves-dropper, and a hitch-hiker. When
Philip caught up with an Ethiopian court official who
was returning from a pilgrimage to Jerusalem, Philip
overheard the man reading aloud from the scriptures.
"Do you understand what you are reading?" Philip
asked him. "How can I unless someone explains it
to me?" the man replied. Philip got in the carriage
and began to interpret the passage from Isaiah. "A
lamb led to the slaughter, silent before his oppressors, deprived of justice and life on earth." Philip said

that this could only refer to Jesus, the crucified Paschal Lamb, whom God raised from the dead. The Ethiopian was so moved he asked to be baptized immediately. Then the man went on his way, rejoicing in his new-found faith. "When I appealed to him in words, praise was on the tip of my tongue," the psalmist declares. Jesus explains that faith is the work of God. All who come to Jesus are drawn by God's grace. The scriptures said that the people could not live on "bread alone," but "by every word that comes forth from the mouth of God" (Deut 8:3). The bread in the wilderness was only a foretaste of the true bread that comes from God. Jesus, the living word of God, is food for our daily journey and for all eternity.

To Consider

- Do I help others understand the scriptures?
- Do I understand them myself?
- Have I availed myself of a good scripture program?

To Pray

Risen Lord, teach me to feed on your life-giving word. Let me be a living gospel to all I meet.

Friday of Third Week of Easter

Jn 6:52–59
  Acts 9:1–20; Ps 117

Unless you eat of the flesh of the Son of Man and drink his blood, you have no life in you. — Jn 6:53

To Note

In John's gospel there is no institution of the Eucharist at the Lord's Supper. That teaching occurs in Jesus' discourse on the "bread of life." In the "wisdom" theme (22–50) the "bread of life" refers to God's revelation in Jesus. In the sacramental theme (51–58), the vocabulary changes to "flesh and blood," "eat and drink." The Greek words for eating are graphic: "to gnaw" or "to munch." Jesus speaks plainly that his flesh is "real food" and his body is "real drink."

To Understand

Later in life, Paul would look back on the incredible events that transformed his life on the road to Damascus. "Why are you persecuting me?" Jesus asked him. By persecuting the church, the body of Christ, Paul was persecuting Jesus. For three days Paul sat in the dark tomb of his own blindness. Ananias, who had heard all about the harm this man had done to his people, was sent by the Lord to heal him. Only God's grace could move Ananias to call Paul his "brother." Paul had breathed murderous threats against the followers of "the new way." Now the life-giving breath of the Spirit inspired Paul to become a follower of Jesus. Paul's heart had been filled with hatred. Now his heart overflowed with the love of Christ. Even Paul's name was changed to signify his new life in Christ. "Praise the Lord, all you nations; the fidelity of the Lord endures forever," the shortest Psalm in the Bible acclaims. Jesus says that God faithfully fed the people throughout their journeys in life. In the wilderness, they ate the "manna" that came down from heaven. Whoever feeds on Jesus' flesh and blood will be transformed by him. They shall not die but live forever. The body of Christ has the power to change the whole world.

To Consider

- As a member of the body of Christ, do I bring healing or hurt?
- How do I show my gratitude for God's good gift?

To Pray

Risen Lord, I praise you for giving us yourself in the Eucharist. I thank you for this life-giving gift.

Saturday of Third Week of Easter

Jn 6:60–69
   Acts 9:31–42; Ps 116

*"Lord, to whom can we go? You have the words of
eternal life." — Jn 6:68*

To Note

The National Catechetical Directory states that the
life of faith is related to human development, which
passes through several stages. "Different people
possess aspects of faith to different degrees" in re-
gard to "the comprehensiveness and intensity with
which they accept God's word, of their ability to
explain it, and of their ability to apply it to life.
Catechesis is meant to help at each stage of human
development and lead ultimately to full identifica-
tion with Jesus" (#174).

To Understand

"Aeneas get up!" "Tabitha rise up!" Aeneas had
been paralyzed, confined to his bed for eight years,
but at Peter's command he stands up. The miracle
of Tabitha's rising is even more incredible. She was
dead. The psalmist asks, "What return can I make to
the Lord for all the good he has done for me?" As
wonderful as these miracles were for Aeneas and
Tabitha, they were more important as signs of Jesus'
life-giving presence in the church. Because of these

signs, many came to believe. Although the signs and wonders that Jesus performed brought many to faith, sometimes his words were hard to swallow. "I am the bread of life," he tells them. Many of his disciples object, "How can anyone take this talk seriously?" "Does it shake your faith?" Jesus asks them. If they cannot believe that he is God's word become flesh, what will they think when he ascends to glory? Jesus refuses to retract his words but invites his followers to a deeper faith. He knows that only God's grace can open their hearts and minds to the mysteries he came to reveal. "What about you?" Jesus directs his question to the Twelve. "Do you want to leave me too?" Peter's answer is faith-filled: "Lord, to whom can we go? You have the words of eternal life. We are convinced that you are God's holy one."

To Consider

• Do I find some of Jesus' statements hard to accept?

• Am I convinced that his words lead to eternal life?

• What will help me grow to a deeper level of faith?

To Pray

Risen Lord, help us to hold fast to the life you have given us so we may receive the eternal gifts you promise.

Fourth Sunday of Easter (ABC)

(A) Jn 10:1–10
    Acts 2:14,36–41; Ps 23; 1 Pet 2:20–25
(B) Jn 10:11–18
    Acts 4:8–12; Ps 118; 1 Jn 3:1–2
(C) Jn 10:27–30
    Acts 13:14,43–52; Ps 100; Rev 7:9,14–17

> *I am the good shepherd. I know my own and my own know me.* — *Jn 10:14*

To Note

The Vatican II "Decree on the Ministry and Life of Priests" states that through the sacrament of Holy Orders, priests share "in the authority by which Christ himself builds up and sanctifies and rules his Body." Through baptism, "all the faithful are made a holy and kingly priesthood"; thus the whole body shares in the one priesthood of Christ in different ways (#2).

To Understand

In the bible, God is often imaged as a shepherd who guides and protects the people when human leaders neglect their welfare or lead them astray. Peter tells the Christian community that at one time they were like straying sheep. Now they have Christ, the "shepherd" and "guardian," as their guide. Jesus says that he is the "good shepherd" who leads the people through the "gate" to the safe pastures and wide horizons of God's kingdom. The false shepherds look after their own interests rather than those of the flock. Jesus gives his life for his followers because he has a personal relationship with each of them. The sheep follow him because his voice is familiar. The love of Jesus is not limited to those who belong to him. It extends to all who are "far off" and have not yet heard his voice. When they are united in his saving love, there will be "one flock" and "one shepherd." In John's "revelation," he sees a huge throng of every nation, race and tongue joyfully acclaiming the "lamb" who is their shepherd. It was in the redeeming blood of the lamb that they have washed their baptismal robes and are victorious. Jesus has led them to the life-giving waters of baptism and has satisfied their hunger and thirst in the Eucharist. Because Jesus has given his life for his followers, they will never perish.

To Consider

- Am I aware that Jesus has called me by name?
- In what ways am I called to serve his flock?
- How is Christ asking me to follow him today?

To Pray

Good Shepherd Jesus, thank you for giving your life for my sake. Help me to hear your call and follow you each day.

Monday of Fourth Week of Easter

Jn 10:1–10 or Jn 10:11–18
    Acts 11:1–18; Ps 42,43

What God has made clean, you must not call profane.
— *Acts 11:9*

To Note

The "Pastoral Constitution on the Church in the
Modern World" states that all people are "endowed
with a rational soul and are created in God's image;
they have the same nature and origin and, being
redeemed by Christ, they enjoy the same divine
calling and destiny." Discrimination in basic human
rights on the grounds of "sex, race, color, social conditions, language or religion, must be curbed and
eradicated as incompatible with God's design" (#29).

To Understand

"You went into *their* house! You ate with *those* people!" The Jerusalem community was incredulous.
How could Peter think of doing such a thing? Why
would he *want* to do such a thing? Peter was as
amazed as they were. It wasn't his idea in the first
place. He simply obeyed the Spirit's call. While he
was at prayer in Joppa, he saw a vision of a large sheet
coming down from the heavens filled with unclean
animals. "Take and eat," a voice commanded. "No
way!" said Peter. "Nothing unclean has ever entered

my mouth and it never will!" The voice was emphatic: "What God has created pure, you are not to call unclean." At the very same time, some men in Caesarea heard another voice command them to go to Joppa and fetch Peter. This time Peter did not argue. Peter entered the "unclean" house in Caesarea and began to preach the gospel. Before he could finish, the Spirit came upon the whole household as on Pentecost. Peter was magnanimous: "If God is giving these Gentiles the same gift that we received, who are we to interfere?" Jesus says that his flock hears his voice and follows him. The sheep will not follow a stranger because they do not recognize his voice. The good shepherd calls each of his own by name. He walks in front of his sheep, leading them to safe pastures where the intolerance of "thieves and marauders" cannot harm them.

To Consider

- What sort of prejudices do I harbor?
- What will help me to see others the way God does?
- Do I listen to Jesus' voice and do what he tells me?

To Pray

Good shepherd Jesus, help me to listen to your voice each day. Help me to be obedient to your call.

Tuesday of Fourth Week of Easter

Jn 10:22–30
  Acts 11:19–26; Ps 87

*It was in Antioch that the disciples were first called
"Christians." — Acts 11:26*

To Note

The "National Catechetical Directory" declares that
"the church continues the mission of Jesus, prophet,
priest, and servant king" with the central purpose of
bringing about God's kingdom. "This one mission
has three aspects: proclaiming and teaching God's
word, celebrating the sacred mysteries, and serving
the people of the world" (#30).

To Understand

After Rome and Alexandria, Antioch was the third
greatest city in the world. It was in Antioch that the
followers of Jesus Christ were first called "Christians." What was it that identified these believers as
belonging to Christ? Most importantly, the church at
Antioch was a community made up of Greeks, Jews
and Roman Christians. In Jesus, they found their
unity and strength and gave witness of this to the
world. When evidence of God's favor in Antioch
reached Jerusalem, the community sent Barnabas to
investigate. Barnabas was the perfect choice, great-
hearted and generous, always ready to take second

place (Acts 4:36–37). Barnabas realized that Paul was the best person for the job of overseeing the Antioch church. Nothing had been heard of Paul since his conversion in Damascus (Acts 9). Now he emerges as the great apostle to the Gentiles. Through Paul and Barnabas, Christianity is launched on its world-wide mission. Jesus says that the works that he does in the Father's name bear witness in his favor. Jesus is the good shepherd who guides his flock into the spacious pastures of the city of God, where all peoples are welcome. The Father has given him these sheep, and no one shall snatch them out of his hand.

To Consider

- Do others recognize me as a Christian?
- What evidence would they have to believe this?
- Do I encourage others to take part in my ministry?

To Pray

Pray Psalm 87 for the needs of all the nations, and pray for the missionaries who have been sent to these lands.

Wednesday of Fourth Week of Easter

Jn 12:44–50
   Acts 12:24–13:5; Ps 67

*Whoever believes in me believes not in me but in him
who sent me. — Jn 12:44*

To Note

The word "liturgy" originally meant "public service." Christians applied the word to their worship, a
service of thanksgiving and praise owed to God. The
liturgy is the public worship shared by the ordained
ministry and the laity. Each has an important role to
play. The entire assembly gathers to remember the
death and resurrection of Christ, to listen to his
words, to respond to God's gift in the sacrament, and
to be sent into the world to proclaim the Lord, who
is present and active among us.

To Understand

The church in Antioch grew in numbers and power.
People from many lands and many backgrounds
found their oneness in Jesus Christ. The leaders of
the community were those who were anointed with
prophetic and teaching gifts. On one occasion, as the
community gathered for the eucharistic liturgy, the
Holy Spirit directed them to set apart Paul and
Barnabas to do the work for which God had called
them. After fasting and praying, the community im-

posed hands on the pair and sent them to take the gospel out into the world. "May all the peoples praise you!" the psalmist exhorts, "May all the ends of the earth fear God." Jesus has been sent into the world as the full revelation of God. Jesus tells his disciples that whoever puts faith in him believes not so much in him as in the one who sent him. The truth that Jesus came to reveal illuminates the world, driving out the darkness of ignorance and sin. Whoever sees Jesus sees the one who sent him. Whoever hears Jesus hears what God has commanded him to speak. Each person has the freedom to accept or reject God's truth. All who refuse to believe bring judgment upon themselves. All who believe in Jesus' life-giving words find eternal life.

To Consider

- In what ways have I been called by God?
- What gifts have I received to do this work?
- How have my words and deeds revealed God's truth?

To Pray

Risen Lord, open my eyes to the light of your truth, which you have made known to us on earth.

Thursday of Fourth Week of Easter

Jn 13:16–20
    Acts 13:13–25; Ps 89

> *Whoever receives one whom I send receives me; and*
> *whoever receives me receives him who sent me.*
> *— Jn 13:20*

To Note

In his encyclical on the church's missionary mandate
("Redemptoris Missio," 1991), Pope John Paul II
says that the mission *ad gentes* (to the people) is still
in its infancy. As the end of the second millennium
of the redemption draws near, the majority of peoples have not yet received the initial proclamation of
Christ. All peoples have a right to receive the proclamation of salvation.

To Understand

Paul and Barnabas have been commissioned by the
community in Antioch to begin their first missionary
journey. Throughout their travels, they herald Jesus
as the fulfillment of God's promise and proclaim a
baptism of repentance for all peoples. John Mark,
Barnabas' cousin, had accompanied the two apostles,
but he suddenly left them in Pamphylia and returned to Jerusalem. Was it cold feet or the hardships
of the journey that made him turn back? Whatever
the reason, it caused such a disagreement between

Barnabas and Paul that the pair separated (Acts 15:39). Though quarrels arise even among the holiest people, reconciliation is always possible. Years later Paul writes from prison, "Get Mark and bring him with you, for he can be of great service to me" (2 Tim 4:11). The great apostle Paul always regarded himself as God's "servant" (Greek *doulos*, Rom 1:1), obedient to the will of the master. Jesus tells his disciples that no slave outranks the master; no messenger is greater than the one who sent him. He demonstrates his servanthood by washing the feet of his disciples (Jn 13:5). Jesus sends his followers into the world to preach a gospel of love and repentance. Whoever accepts those he sends accepts Jesus and the one who sent him.

To Consider

- How have I proclaimed the good news today?
- Am I willing to forgive those who have forsaken me?
- Do I aspire to be a servant or a master of others?

To Pray

Risen Lord, make me worthy to preach your holy gospel. I pray for all who proclaim your word to the world.

Friday of Fourth Week of Easter

Jn 14:1–6
   Acts 13:26–33; Ps 2

I am the way, and the truth, and the life. — Jn 14:6

To Note

When Jesus declares that he is the "way, the truth and the life," he echoes concepts from the Hebrew Scriptures. The psalmist prays, "Teach me, O Lord, your *way* that I may walk in your *truth*" (Ps 86:11) and again, "You show me the path of *life*" (Ps 16:11). Jesus reveals that the way to God's truth and eternal life is by following his path to Calvary.

To Understand

Paul and Barnabas arrive in Antioch in Pisidia, a territory in Phrygia (not Antioch in Syria, where they departed on their missionary journey, Acts 13:1–4). Paul tells the people the good news and the bad news. The bad news is that they have lost their way. Although they have heard the words of the prophets read to them sabbath after sabbath, they failed to recognize their fulfillment in Jesus Christ. The good news is that God has shown them the way by fulfilling the promises made to their ancestors. The pledge made to David, "You are my son; today I have begotten you" (Ps 2:7), was accomplished in the dying and rising of Jesus. Before his death, Jesus foretold what would happen to him, yet his disciples failed to understand his words. As he prepares to depart from this world, Jesus consoles his troubled followers, telling them to have faith in his promises. Jesus is the faithful Son who came to reveal the way to God the Father. Now he goes to prepare a dwelling place for his followers where they can live with him for eternity. Jesus is confident that his disciples understand where he is going, but they wonder: "Is there a way?...Can we find the way?" Thomas verbalizes their concern: "How can we know the way?" Jesus assures them that he *is* the way to all truth and to unending life with God.

To Consider

- Do I find life in Jesus' words?
- What is my understanding of "truth"?
- How can I help others find the way to truth and life?

To Pray

Risen Lord, you show me the path to truth. With you we have the fullness of life.

Saturday of Fourth Week of Easter

Jn 14:7–14
   Acts 13:44–52; Ps 98

Believe me that I am in the Father and the Father is in me; but if you do not, then believe because of the works themselves. — Jn 14:11

To Note

The word "revelation" means "taking away the veil" that prevents God's self-disclosure. Throughout salvation history, God was revealed through words and deeds. In his incarnation, life, teachings, works, death and resurrection, Jesus was the divine revealer, the full revelation of the message of God. This manifestation of God invites a personal response of faith and acceptance of revealed truth.

To Understand

When Paul and Barnabas preached in Antioch in Pisidia, they attracted great crowds, but they also drew a lot of fire. Those who were jealous of their success countered with violent abuse. Some of them incited the influential men and women of the city to take action against the pair. Paul fearlessly confronted his adversaries. Since they rejected God's word, they convicted themselves as being unworthy of God's gift of everlasting life. Rebuffed by their own people, Paul and Barnabas turn to the Gentiles, who accept their message wholeheartedly. The apostles are filled with joy as the Spirit inspires them to preach the word of God in other lands. The psalmist sings joyfully, "All the ends of the earth have seen the salvation of God." Jesus tells his followers that he does not act on his own. It is the Father who speaks and works through him. If they really understood who Jesus was, they would hear and see the Father. The disciples fail to comprehend his words and Philip demands, "Show us the Father." Jesus says that his words and deeds have revealed the Father. If they cannot believe what he tells them, at least they can have faith in what he does. The Holy Spirit will empower those who have faith in Jesus to accomplish even greater works.

To Consider

- How has God been revealed to me today?
- In what ways have I seen the Spirit working?
- Have my words and deeds revealed Christ to others?

To Pray

Risen Lord, help me to understand what you reveal to us about God. Help me to hear your voice and see your works in the words and deeds of your people.

Fifth Sunday of Easter (ABC)

(A) Jn 14:1–12
    Acts 6:1–7; Ps 33; 1 Pet 2:4–9
(B) Jn 15:1–8
    Acts 9:26–31; Ps 22; 1 Jn 3:18–24
(C) Jn 13:31–33,34–35
    Acts 14:21–27; Ps 145; Rev 21:1–5

I am the true vine, and my Father is the vine grower.
— Jn 15:1

To Note

In 325 CE, the Council of Nicaea addressed the doctrine of the Trinity in response to the Arian heresy that threatened the unity of the church. Arius taught that Jesus was not divine by nature, but merely the first of God's created beings. Under the leadership of Athanasius, bishop of Alexander, the council affirmed that Christ was of "the same substance" (Greek *homoousios*, "consubstantial") and equal with the Father.

To Understand

As the church of Jerusalem grew in numbers and diversity, it suffered growing pains. When the community was ethnically and culturally alike, things were harmonious. When the community grew beyond these familial bonds, dissension began to erupt. John addresses the problems of his own community.

Some refused to acknowledge that Jesus was the Christ, and others denied that he was true man. The Spirit of the risen Lord is the binding force that preserves the unity. Peter compares Christ to the "cornerstone," upon which the whole church is constructed. Believers are "living stones," built into a sacred temple. Jesus says that there is plenty of room in God's house for all to worship. He compares himself to a vine to show how his disciples must draw life from him. God the Father is the "vine grower" who prunes away the lifeless branches in order to increase their fruitfulness. In John's "revelation" the church is represented as a beautiful bride coming down from heaven to meet Christ, her bridegroom. John sees "new heavens" and a "new earth" in which all people dwell as one. If all people follow Christ's command to "love one another," the world will believe that God dwells in their midst.

To Consider

- Is my parish a place of love and unity or of alienation and division?
- What are the dead branches that need to be pruned?

To Pray

Risen Lord, help your church to bring about a "new earth" of peace and justice. Help us to love others as you do.

Monday of Fifth Week of Easter

Jn 14:21–26
    Acts 14:5–18; Ps 115

> *The Advocate, the holy Spirit, whom the Father will
> send in my name, will teach you everything, and remind
> you of all that I have said to you. — Jn 14:26*

To Note

The Holy Spirit is our "paraclete" (Greek *parakaleo*,
Latin *ad-vocatus*, "advocate"), a legal term for one
who "stands beside another" to defend and to help
in times of trial. The divinity of the Spirit was proclaimed at the First Council of Constantinople in 381
CE. Our Creed states that the Spirit "proceeds" from
the Father and the Son and is worshiped and glorified "with" the Father and the Son.

To Understand

"Stand up!" Paul commanded the lame man. The
man had been crippled from birth, and Paul expected him to stand? But the man not only stood, he
walked and leaped! When the crowds saw what happened they thought that the gods had come to visit
them. They figured that Barnabas was Zeus, the king
of the Greek gods, and Paul was Hermes, the messenger of the gods. The distressed apostles objected,
"We are only human like you." Barnabas *was* a man
of great nobility; he had been generous to Paul and

to the church. Paul *was* a messenger, not of false gods, but of the living God, creator of all things. The psalmist affirms that "idols are silver and gold, the handiwork of men," but the "Lord has made heaven and earth." Jesus is the supreme messenger of the good news. The word that he speaks is not his own; it comes from the one true God, who sent him. The unbelieving world cannot accept what he says because they do not love Jesus nor keep his commandments. All who love Jesus will be true to his revealed word, and they will be loved by God. The Father and Son will find a dwelling place in the hearts of these faithful ones. Though Jesus' followers cannot fully understand what he has taught them, God will send the Holy Spirit, who will instruct them in everything and remind them of all that he has said.

To Consider

- What are the false "gods" that I venerate?
- How can I rid myself of this deception?
- How can I show obedience to God's word today?

To Pray

Father and Son, make me a worthy temple of your Holy Spirit. I love you and want to be true to your commands.

Tuesday of Fifth Week of Easter

Jn 14:27–31
  Acts 14:19–28; Ps 145

Peace I leave with you; my peace I give to you.
— *Jn 14:27*

To Note

The United States Bishops' Pastoral Statement,
"The Challenge of Peace: God's Promise and Our
Response," states that "peacemaking is not an op-
tional commitment. It is a requirement of our faith."
The risen Christ "sustains us in confronting the
awesome challenge of the nuclear arms race," and he
asks us to "take responsibility for his work of creation
and try to shape it in the ways of the Kingdom"
(1983).

To Understand

Paul's enemies viciously stoned him and left him for
dead, but his faithful disciples formed a protective
circle around him until he could recover. That experience didn't stop Paul. The next day he and
Barnabas continued their proclamation of the good
news in many places. Before the apostles left each
community, they installed elders to care for the community. The apostles knew the young church would
encounter persecution and opposition as they had,
and they encouraged the faithful to persevere in

their fidelity to Christ. When Paul and Barnabas finished their first missionary journey, they returned to Antioch and gathered the congregation together to tell them all that God had accomplished through them. "Let all your works give you thanks, O Lord, and let your faithful ones bless you," the psalmist enjoins. As Jesus prepares to leave his disciples, he gives them a farewell gift of "peace" (Hebrew *shalom*). The peace that Jesus imparts is not only the cessation of hostilities but the abiding presence of the Spirit in the midst of the turmoil and conflicts of this world. Though the enemy is close at hand, Jesus is in control of his own destiny. His followers will rejoice when they understand that he has left this world in love and obedience to God's will.

To Consider

- Am I a gift of peace to others or a source of discord?
- To whom do I need to offer Christ's peace today?
- What area of my life needs peace?

To Pray

Risen Lord, make me an instrument of your peace so that your kingdom will triumph over all injustice.

Wednesday of Fifth Week of Easter

Jn 15:1–8
  Acts 15:1–6; Ps 122

Just as the branch cannot bear fruit by itself unless it abides in the vine, neither can you unless you abide in me. — Jn 15:4

To Note

The magisterium (Latin, "office of teacher") is the official teaching body of the church. While all baptized Christians have the obligation of announcing the good news, the magisterium has the unique responsibility of teaching the church's doctrine. This magisterial authority belongs to the college of bishops (the apostolic successors) united with the Bishop of Rome. Guided by the Spirit, the magisterium interprets Christ's saving truth and applies it to the new challenges of each age.

To Understand

When Jesus left this earthly life, he didn't leave a rule book behind. "Just look up ordinance number 49 and it will tell you what to do in this situation." Jesus simply told his followers to stay connected to him. He was the vine; they were the branches. In union with Christ, the church would draw its life from him and would be fruitful. Apart from him they would be ineffective. Jesus said that God is the vine grower who trims the branches, pruning the barren ones to increase their yield. Pruning hurts, but it is necessary if the vine is to be healthy and productive. As the church grew in numbers and diversity, the leaders realized that there was a lot of dead wood around. While circumcision was a valuable tradition for the Jewish Christians, it was meaningless for the Gentiles. Some Judean Christians insisted that circumcision remain a condition for the Gentiles to come into the church. Paul and Barnabas disagreed with them; all were at a deadlock. If only Jesus was here to decide the issue! But the risen Christ was present and active in the church. Paul and Barnabas decided to take the matter to the apostles and elders in the Jerusalem church and let them resolve the argument. With the Spirit's guidance, the church would know the mind of Christ.

To Consider

- Do I look to the church for guidance in my moral and spiritual life?
- What part does conscience play?
- Is my ministry fruitful or unproductive?

To Pray

Risen Lord, guide your church in all of its decisions. Prune away anything that keeps your people from being fruitful.

Thursday of Fifth Week of Easter

Jn 15:9–11
  Acts 15:7–21; Ps 96

As the Father has loved me, so I have loved you; abide in my love. — Jn 15:9

To Note

Grace (Greek *charis*, "gift") is the unmerited favor God bestows on humanity. Divine grace was manifested in God's covenant with the chosen people, and it was continually offered despite their disobedience. The fullness of God's grace was granted through Jesus' saving death, which shows the wideness of God's love for all people. Baptism is a means of grace by which Christians are undeservedly justified before God. Through the gift of the Spirit, grace continues to operate in the life of the believer.

To Understand

Paul and Barnabas had a dilemma to resolve. Should circumcision be required of Gentile Christians or not? The apostles took the dispute to Jerusalem for a decision. After much debate, Peter took the floor and reminded them how he had been a missionary to the Gentiles from the earliest days. He recalled how the Spirit acted in the case of the Gentile Cornelius (Acts 10). The Law declared this man to be ritually unclean, but God decided otherwise. The gift of God was not for a select few but for all. Peter went to the heart of the matter: "Why do you place a burden on these new converts that we did not bear? It is our belief that we are all saved by God's grace, not by any merit of our own." After Paul and Barnabas shared how God's favor had been granted to the Gentiles, James, another "pillar" in the Jerusalem church (Gal 2:9), spoke up. James suggested that in charity, the Gentiles should observe a few regulations that would ease their relationships with the Jewish Christians allowing them to live in peace and accord. Before his death and resurrection, Jesus told his disciples to keep the spirit of God's commands. If they live in love with one another, they will enjoy communion with the Father, Son, and Spirit.

To Consider

- Do I take into account how my decisions will affect others?
- Am I fair to all?
- Do I obey God's commands in the spirit of love?

To Pray

Risen Lord, guide your leaders to make wise decisions that will bring peace and justice to all peoples.

Friday of Fifth Week of Easter

Jn 15:12–17
  Acts 15:22–31; Ps 57

You are my friends if you do what I command you.
— Jn 15:14

To Note

The pope (Greek, "father"), the vicar of Jesus Christ, is the head of the Catholic church. As Peter's successor, the Bishop of Rome is a visible sign of Christ's authority on earth. The First Vatican Council defined the papal office in terms of universal jurisdiction and infallibility. Vatican II expressed the collegial character of the papacy exercised with all bishops. In the sixth century, Pope Gregory the Great, Doctor of the church, chose as his title, "The Servant of the servants of God," a motto still in use today.

To Understand

After the debate over circumcision was resolved by the Jerusalem council, representatives of the community were sent to Antioch along with Paul and Barnabas. These leaders, Judas Barsabas and Silas, were to read a letter to the community which clarified the matter. "It is the decision of the Holy Spirit and ours," the letter announced, "that no unnecessary burdens be laid upon the Gentile Christians with the exception of those regulations which promote harmony between them and the Jewish Christians." The church at Antioch was delighted that peace had returned to their community. Before Jesus departed from this world, he told his apostles that the supreme commandment is the law of love, and that their role as apostles is one of service. Jesus did not ask them to do something he was not willing to do himself, and he asks them to imitate his example of loving service (Jn 13). Jesus will prove his love by laying down his life for the world. Jesus has shared everything he has received from the Father with the apostles. Because they have intimate knowledge of him, they are his friends. Slaves do not have this kind of relationship with their masters. Jesus has chosen his apostles to go forth and proclaim the gospel of love to the world. Their labors will be fruitful if they are obedient to Jesus' command to love.

To Consider

- Do I feel like a slave or a friend of Jesus?
- How have I obeyed his command to love today?
- Do I do this with joy or out of obligation?

To Pray

Risen Lord, thank you for giving your life for me and teaching me how to love. Help me to love as you do.

Saturday of Fifth Week of Easter

Jn 15:18–21
   Acts 16:1–10; Ps 100

Come over to Macedonia and help us. — Acts 16:9

To Note

In his encyclical "Redemptoris Missio: on the Permanent Validity of the Church's Missionary Mandate (1991)," Pope John Paul II said that we need to be attentive to those parts of the world which have not felt the influence of the gospel. All the faithful should have an apostolic zeal to share their light and joy.

To Understand

Paul won the battle that declared circumcision unnecessary for the Gentiles (Acts 15:11), but he lost the battle with Barnabas, his friend and companion. After a heated argument as to whether they should take John Mark on their second missionary journey, the two apostles parted and Paul went his own way (Acts 15:36–40). When Paul met Timothy, he saw the young man as a possible associate and invited him to come along. The next generation must be trained to preach the gospel to the world. Because Timothy was a son of a mixed marriage (Jew and Gentile), the young man had never been circumcised. While circumcision was not required of the

Gentiles, it was for Jews. Paul had Timothy circumcised to make him acceptable as a missionary to his people. On their travels, Paul was prevented from preaching in Asia Minor. At first this appeared to be a setback, but the Spirit is always ready to move in a different direction. Paul was called to the province of Macedonia, where he established the first mission on European soil. Jesus chose his friends to share in the work of evangelization. He warned his followers of the difficulties they would face. If the world refused to listen to him, would his disciples fare any better? The servants will share in the suffering of the master as they labor to make the world one.

To Consider

- Does fear of rejection keep me from speaking the truth?
- Am I able to change my course when my plans fail?
- Do I follow the lead of the Holy Spirit?

To Pray

Risen Lord, help me to break down the barriers that separate your people. Help me to show them your love.

Sixth Sunday of Easter (ABC)

(A) Jn 14:15–21
     Acts 8:5–8,14–17; Ps 66; 1 Pet 3:15–18
(B) Jn 15:9–17
     Acts 10:25–26,34–35,44–48; Ps 98; 1 Jn 4:7–10
(C) John 14:23–29
     Acts 15:1–2,22–29; Ps 67; Rev 21:10–14,22–23

This I command you: love one another. — Jn 15:17

To Note

One of the most remarkable definitions of the church that came out of Vatican II was "the people of God." "The Dogmatic Constitution of the Church" declared that God has willed to save people, "not as individuals without any bond or link between them, but rather to make them into a people." This people bears witness to Christ by serving one another in faith, love and holiness (#9, 12).

To Understand

How does the church remain faithful to the vision of Jesus as circumstances change? This was the problem faced by the early church. When Peter stepped over the threshold of the home of Cornelius, an "unclean" Gentile, a new age in the church began. The Holy Spirit poured forth upon the Gentiles, and Peter declared, "I can see now that God has no favorites. People of every nation are acceptable to

166

God." Some argued that unless the Gentiles were circumcised, God could not save them. At Jerusalem, it was unanimously resolved that no burden should be laid on people who did not share their religious tradition. The church leaders did not make this decision on their own. The Spirit acted in them and guided their judgment. John addresses problems in his own divided community. He says that the ability to love not only comes from God, it is God's very nature: "God *is* love." Those who do not love know nothing of God. Before Jesus left this earth, he gave his disciples a simple command: "Love one another." Obeying his commands would not be a burdensome task if they did it with love. Though Jesus would no longer be physically present to assist them, he would not leave them orphans; the "Spirit of truth" would be present in the community to guide and instruct them.

To Consider

- What is my attitude toward people who are different than myself—in race, nationality, religion or gender?
- What attitude adjustments do I need to make?
- How can the Spirit help me to do this?

To Pray

Risen Lord, send your Spirit to unite all your people. Help us to practice the faith that we profess.

Monday of Sixth Week of Easter

Jn 15:26–16:4
   Acts 16:11–15; Ps 149

*You also are to testify, because you have been with me
from the beginning. — Jn 15:27*

To Note

In his apostolic exhortation, "Evangelization in the
Modern World," Pope Paul VI said that "Jesus himself, the Good News of God, was the first and foremost evangelist," and that the "Holy Spirit is the
principal agent of evangelization" who "inspires
each individual to proclaim the Gospel." It is also the
Spirit "who causes the word of salvation to be understood and accepted" (1975).

To Understand

"*We* put out to sea." The abrupt change in language
from singular to plural may indicate that Luke, the
author of the Gospel and the Acts of the Apostles,
may have joined Paul on his mission to Europe. (An
interesting conjecture is that Luke may have been
the one who invited Paul to "come over to Macedonia" [v 9].) When the evangelists arrive in Philippi,
an important city in Macedonia, they go to a well-
known "place of prayer" by the river and speak to
the women who are gathered there. Lydia, a prominent, "God-fearing" businesswoman, is convinced

by Paul's preaching and is baptized. In gratitude, she offers the hospitality of her home to the missionaries. As Jesus prepares to face suffering and death, he tells his followers that they will not always be welcomed by those to whom they have been sent. There will be those who expel them from their places of prayer. Others will claim that they are serving God by putting them to death. Nevertheless, the apostles have been eye-witnesses to Jesus' works and teachings, and they *must* bear witness on his behalf. Jesus promises that the Holy Spirit will strengthen them in the face of hostility. The Spirit will testify to the truth of their message and will preserve the validity of Jesus' words throughout the ages.

To Consider

- Am I able to convince others of the truth of the gospel?
- Can I do this with love and respect?
- How have I experienced the Holy Spirit in these moments?

To Pray

Risen Lord, send your Spirit to speak your words of truth through me. Let me bear witness to you in spite of ill will.

Tuesday of Sixth Week of Easter

Jn 16:5–11
Acts 16:22–34; Ps 138

When [the Spirit] comes, he will prove the world wrong about sin and righteousness and judgment. — Jn 16:8

To Note

The United States Bishops' "Pastoral Statement on World Mission" (1986) states that those who have not heard the gospel are often "doubly poor, doubly hungry, doubly oppressed." The importance of responding to these human needs is stressed in another document, "Instruction on Christian Freedom and Liberation." The Lord has entrusted the church with "the word of truth which is capable of enlightening consciences"; therefore, "Divine love impels her to a true solidarity with everyone who suffers."

To Understand

A demented slave girl followed Paul around shouting, "These people are slaves of the Most High God, who proclaim to you a way of salvation." Her words are true; the missionaries *are* God's servants who proclaim the way to salvation, but Paul was annoyed by her incessant shouting, and he exorcised the spirit of insanity which held her in bondage. Some unscrupulous men who used the girl for fortune telling become enraged when their source of revenue was lost. They stirred up the crowd and Paul and Silas were arrested. While the two missionaries prayed and sang hymns, an earthquake shook the place and the prison doors swung open. Their jailer was also shaken to his foundation, and he asked the missionaries what he could do to be saved. Their answer was that it is not in the doing but in believing in Jesus Christ. The jailer and his whole household are baptized, and they celebrate their newfound faith with a meal. In the eyes of the world, Jesus was put on trial, was found guilty, and died in disgrace. But the Spirit proves the world wrong, and the judgment is reversed. The Spirit acts as an advocate of those who are falsely accused and prosecutes those who refuse to believe the truth. The ruler of darkness is the one who is tried, convicted and condemned. In the end truth will triumph, and justice will prevail.

To Consider

- In what ways do I participate in the liberation of those who are oppressed?
- Do I stand up for truth in spite of the consequences?
- How has the Spirit strengthened me in this task?

To Pray

Risen Lord, help me to speak the truth that sets people free.

Wednesday of Sixth Week of Easter

Jn 16:12–15
> Acts 17:15,22–18:1; Ps 148

*When the Spirit of truth comes, he will guide you into
all the truth. — Jn 16:13*

To Note

Pope Paul VI declared that "there is no true evangelization if the name, the teaching, the life, the
promises, the kingdom and the mystery of Jesus of
Nazareth, the Son of God, are not proclaimed." He
said that the center of the message is "the clear
proclamation that in Jesus Christ...salvation is offered to every human being" (Evangelization in the
Modern World).

To Understand

When Paul arrived in Athens, he became exasper-
ated by the sight of so many idols. He tried to debate
with some of the Epicurean and Stoic philosophers,
but they mocked him. The Epicureans believed that
death ended everything, so they indulged their ap-
petites in material pleasures. The Stoics, on the
other hand, were indifferent to the material world
and followed a life of virtue and reason. The philosophers took Paul to the Areopagus (Greek, "Mars
Hill"), where he was asked to state his "strange
notions" before the learned citizens. Paul appealed

to their belief in a divine creator of the universe and to their attempt to find God in the natural world. Paul even quoted from one of their poets, but he had little success in converting them. Later, Paul resolves to "preach nothing but Jesus Christ crucified" (1 Cor 2:2). As Jesus prepares to suffer and die, he consoles his grieving followers with the promise of the Holy Spirit. Although they have not been able to comprehend everything that Jesus has taught them, the Spirit will guide them to the truth. Those things that perplex them now will be clarified by the Spirit. Just as Jesus spoke only the words that the Father communicated to him, the Spirit will interpret Jesus' message for all generations.

To Consider

- Do I try to modify my beliefs when I speak to others?
- Am I afraid that I will be mocked for my convictions?
- How does the Spirit help me?

To Pray

Risen Lord, send your Spirit to guide and direct the teaching of the church. Announce your words of truth to the world.

Thursday of Sixth Week of Easter

Note: This Mass is celebrated in those places where the celebration of the Ascension is transferred to the Seventh Sunday of Easter.

Jn 16:16–20
   Acts 18:1–8; Ps 98

A little while, and you will no longer see me, and again a little while, and you will see me. — Jn 16:16

To Note

The Didache (Greek, "teaching") is among the oldest writings of the church. This document, titled "The Teachings of the Twelve Apostles," was compiled from various sources toward the end of the first century by an anonymous Jewish-Christian author. The work is a statement of Christian beliefs concerning the ways that lead to life or death, instruction on baptism, the Eucharist, fasting, and prayer.

To Understand

Jesus told his grieving disciples, "Within a short time you will lose sight of me, but soon you will see me again." His confused followers asked one another, "What can he mean? What is this 'short time'? We don't know what he's talking about." Although Jesus would vanish from their sight in his ascension to God, he makes his presence known in those who preach and teach the gospel. Paul was one of those whom the Lord called to carry the good news to the world. Paul found himself going from one city to the next as he travelled on his missionary journeys. When he was rejected in one place, he went on to another. Paul was not alone in his work. There were many men and women, Jews and Gentiles, who assisted him: Aquila and his wife Priscilla, Silas and Timothy, Titus Justus and others. Like Jesus, Paul found lodging with whomever welcomed him. At times Paul found it necessary to support himself, so he took up tentmaking alongside Priscilla and Aquila. At other times he totally devoted himself to preaching the gospel. Jesus was alive in the hearts of those who heard God's word. Though Jesus' followers wept and mourned when he departed, their grief was turned to joy when they saw and heard him in the deeds and teachings of the church.

To Consider

- Am I persistent in sharing the good news even when I am rejected?
- Am I hospitable to those who teach and preach God's word?
- Do I support them financially?

To Pray

Risen Lord, help me to see you when I lose sight of you. Help me to hear your words in the gospel.

Ascension of the Lord (ABC)

Note: In some places, the celebration of the Ascension is transferred to the Seventh Sunday of Easter.

(A) Mt 28:16–20
    (ABC) Acts 1:1–11; Ps 47; Eph 1:17–23
(B) Mk 16:15–20
(C) Lk 24:46–53

I am with you always, to the end of the age. — *Mt 28:20*

To Note

The ascension was the sign and seal of Christ's earthly work of salvation. The Acts of the Apostles shows forty days of appearances of the risen Christ as a prelude to the sending of the Spirit. The essence of the ascension is Christ's exaltation and enthronement at the "right hand of God" and his priestly reign in power and authority (Mk 16:19; Heb 4:14). Christ is still with us today in the teaching, preaching, sacraments and institutions of the church.

To Understand

Jesus did not abandon his followers when he ascended to heaven. Though it was necessary for him to suffer, die and rise from the dead "for the remission of sins," Jesus pledges his abiding presence in the church. He summons those he has chosen to the mountain and empowers them with the "full authority" (Greek *exousia*) that he himself has received from God. The apostles were eye-witnesses to the life and death of Jesus, and now they must carry on his mission. Before his departure, Jesus imparts a blessing and a promise to send the Spirit to "clothe them with power from on high." Just as Jesus shares God's authority, so too are the "immeasurable riches of his grace" in those who believe (Eph 2:7). After the ascension, God's messengers ask Jesus' followers, "Why do you stand there looking up? Get your heads out of the clouds and get busy on earth." The good news of salvation must be proclaimed to all the world. When the apostles go forth as Christ commanded, they encounter him in the many signs that accompany their work. Whoever believes their word and is baptized experiences Christ's saving power.

To Consider

- How have I experienced the risen Christ in my daily life?
- Have I obeyed his command to teach others the good news?
- Do I wait for the Spirit before beginning Christ's work?

To Pray

Risen Lord, may we find hope in your glory as we follow you into your kingdom.

Friday of Sixth Week of Easter

Jn 16:20–23
    Acts 18:9–18; Ps 47

> *I will see you again, and your hearts will rejoice, and*
> *no one will take your joy from you.* — Jn 16:22

To Note

The days between the ascension of the Lord and
Pentecost have been traditionally set aside as a no-
vena in preparation for the feast commemorating the
outpouring of the Holy Spirit on the church. These
nine (Latin *novem*) days of prayer had their origin
when the men and women disciples gathered with
Mary and the apostles to await the promise of the
Holy Spirit (Acts 1:13–14,2:1–4).

To Understand

Paul gave birth to the Christian community in
Corinth, but he was distressed when his work was
met with rejection. Paul received encouragement in
a vision of the risen Lord: "Don't be afraid! Don't
stop speaking! I am with you!" While there were
many of Christ's people in the city who supported
Paul, there were those who turned against him, ac-
cusing him of teaching "ways that are against the
law." Paul was brought to court, but Gallio, a Roman
official, dismissed the case as a religious problem
having nothing to do with Roman justice. The risen

Christ was with Paul as he continued to teach the word of God. After a year and a half, Paul left for Syria in the company of Priscilla and her husband Aquila, his companions in work and ministry. Later, Paul wrote two letters (probably more) to correct problems in the Corinthian church. The Spirit continued to guide the church through the oral and written word. Before Jesus departed from the world, he told his disciples that their grief would turn to joy at his return. He compared their present suffering to a woman giving birth. When a child is brought into the world, she remembers the agony no longer. Though his disciples are in pain now, they will rejoice when they behold the birthing of the kingdom of God.

To Consider

- In what ways have I been consoled by the Lord in difficult circumstances?
- How was this problem resolved?
- In what ways did the Spirit guide me?

To Pray

Risen Lord, give me peace and encouragement in the midst of my afflictions. Send your Spirit to comfort and direct me.

Saturday of Sixth Week of Easter

Jn 16:23–28
    Acts 18:23–28; Ps 47

*Ask and you will receive, so that your joy may be
complete. — Jn 16:24*

To Note

The National Catechetical Directory says that the
source and content of catechesis is one: "God's word,
fully revealed in Jesus Christ and at work in the lives
of people exercising their faith" under the guidance
of the church. Catechesis seeks "to make the biblical
signs better understood, so that people may more
fully live the message of the Bible," and seeks to
encourage people to use the Bible "as a source and
inspiration for prayer" (#41, 42).

To Understand

How often do you hear people say, "When I get to
heaven, the first thing I want is answers to my questions"? Jesus tells us that on that day we will have no
questions. When we see him face to face, all of the
dilemmas that perplex us will pale in significance.
But while we are on earth, the questions and the
problems remain. Jesus tells us to present our needs
to God in his name, and divine wisdom will grant
what is determined to be good for us. Though Jesus
is our intercessor, there is no need for him to petition

on our behalf. God loves us and already knows our needs. Jesus has come to reveal the loving-kindness of God. When Jesus returns to God, those things which seemed veiled and confusing will be fully revealed by the Spirit. Apollos was a man who thought he had all the answers. In his spiritual fervor, he taught scripture and instructed people on the new way of the Lord. Although he was eloquent and fearless, Priscilla and Aquila knew that something was missing in his teaching. Apollos only knew of John's baptism and not baptism in Christ, so Priscilla and Aquila instructed him in greater depth. Fully catechized, Apollos went about preaching that Jesus is the fulfillment of God's promise of the Messiah in the scriptures.

To Consider

- If I could ask God one question, what would it be?
- Would I be satisfied with asking just one?
- What will help me to turn to God with faith and trust?

To Pray

Risen Lord, help us to grow in understanding of the eternal mystery of your death and resurrection. Help us to live it daily.

Seventh Sunday of Easter (ABC)

Note: In some places, the celebration of the Ascension is transferred to the Seventh Sunday of Easter.

(A) Jn 17:1–11
    Acts 1:12–14; Ps 27; 1 Pet 4:13–16
(B) Jn 17:11–19
    Acts 1:15–17,20–26; Ps 103; 1 Jn 4:11–16
(C) Jn 17:20–26
    Acts 7:55–60; Ps 97; Rev 22:12–14,16–17,20

As you have sent me into the world, so I have sent them into the world. — Jn 17:18

To Note

Jesus' prayer of petition for the church in John's gospel has been called the "high priestly prayer," as Jesus prepares to offer himself as victim for the salvation of the world. This longest of Jesus' prayers bears a resemblance to the "Lord's prayer," as Jesus prays to his "Father" in heaven for the kingdom to come on earth.

To Understand

As Jesus is about to fulfill his mission on earth, he gathers his disciples in prayer one last time. On the threshold of eternity, Jesus speaks as though his work is already complete. Jesus knows that his "hour" has come, the moment when he will be

182

glorified by God. He has accomplished the work that has been given him by God. Through his words and deeds, he has revealed to his disciples the one, merciful, ever-present God who is "Father." Jesus has proclaimed God's glory; now he prays for those who will glorify him by continuing his work on earth. Jesus prays that these chosen ones will reveal the love and unity that he shares with God. Before Jesus ascends to glory, he assures his followers that he will not abandon them. They will receive power and authority from the Holy Spirit to be his witnesses to the ends of the earth. After Jesus' death and resurrection, the apostles return to Jerusalem, where they gather in an upper room to pray with Mary and some other disciples of the Lord for the coming of the Spirit. The members of the Christian community are authentic messengers when the world sees that they are united in Christ's sacrificial love. With Mary and all the saints we continue to pray: *Maranatha!* "Come Lord Jesus!"

To Consider

- Do I faithfully gather with the Christian community in prayer?
- Do I pray for the Spirit to direct the church?

To Pray

Come Holy Spirit, fill the hearts of your faithful, and enkindle in them the fire of your love.

Monday of Seventh Week of Easter

Jn 16:29–33
    Acts 19:1–8; Ps 68

> *Did you receive the Holy Spirit when you became believers? — Acts 19:2*

To Note

The Vatican II "Decree on the church's Missionary Activity" states that throughout the ages the Holy Spirit makes the church "one in communion and ministry; and provides her with different hierarchical and charismatic gifts giving life to ecclesiastical structures, being as it were their soul, and inspiring in the hearts of the faithful that same spirit of mission which impelled Christ himself" (#4).

To Understand

"We've never heard of the Holy Spirit!" some disciples told Paul when he asked them if they had received the Spirit when they became believers. The Spirit has been described as the "invisible" person of the Trinity. Perhaps it has something to do with the nature of the Spirit who is transparent and inconspicuous. Fatherhood and sonship is a concept we can grasp, but uncreated grace is something we have difficulty comprehending. It is only by experiencing the transforming effects of the Spirit in our lives that it can be appreciated. Before the disciples received the fullness of the Spirit on Pentecost, they had trouble understanding Jesus' teachings. It was as though he spoke in "veiled language." On the eve of his crucifixion, Jesus tried to help them grasp the meaning of the journey he was about to undertake. Though they assumed that they understood his mission, they were naive. Jesus warned them that during his passion they would all scatter like frightened sheep deprived of their shepherd. Even though his followers will desert him, God can never abandon him. The Father and Jesus are one. Jesus tells them this not so they will despair, but that they will take heart. In the world they will suffer greatly, but Jesus has overcome the world and they will share in his victory. On that day, they will have the peace that comes from God's spirit.

To Consider

- What is my experience of the Holy Spirit?
- How has the Spirit given me direction in my life?
- How does the Spirit help me to overcome my problems?

To Pray

Risen Lord, we pray for the life and holiness that comes through the working of the Holy Spirit.

Tuesday of Seventh Week of Easter

Jn 17:1–11
   Acts 20:17–27; Ps 68

*I glorified you on earth by finishing the work that you
gave me to do.* — Jn 17:4

To Note

Chronos and *Kairos* are two ways to measure time.
Chronos is "clock" or "calendar" time. It refers to the
minutes, hours, days, weeks, months and years that
mark our ordinary life. Chronos is horizontal time
whereas Kairos is vertical time. Kairos is the moment
when God's saving action penetrates the world. Kairos time expresses the full scope of God's plan and
purpose in the world.

To Understand

"I'm going to Jerusalem," Paul told the elders of
Ephesus. "I don't know what's going to happen to
me when I get there, but I am compelled by the
Spirit to go." Paul thought he had his life all laid out
for him. An educated man of the world, a devout and
faithful Jew, Paul was certain about his future. Then
a man from Galilee entered his life and upset his
plans. Everything changed for Paul. His security, his
faith and his fortune were turned topsy-turvy. Now
he no longer conducted his affairs according to his
own designs; he let the Spirit guide his life. As Paul

bid farewell to the church of Ephesus, he knew that his conscience was clear. He would finish the course that the Holy Spirit had laid out for him, and he would not shrink from announcing God's reign no matter what price he would be asked to pay. Jesus also says farewell to his beloved companions. He knows that the "hour" of his death has arrived. By dying to his earthly life, Jesus will give eternal life to those who have faith. Jesus did not retreat from his destiny in Jerusalem, but steadfastly set his foot on the road toward it. He has completed the work that God has assigned to him, and now he prays for all those who, like Paul, will continue his work throughout the ages to come.

To Consider

- If I knew that I was facing death, what would I want to say to my loved ones?
- Can I tell them these things now?
- How will the Spirit assist me?

To Pray

Holy Spirit, guide us each day on the path you have set for us. Give us courage to overcome all obstacles that stand in the way of God's kingdom.

Wednesday of Seventh Week of Easter

Jn 17:11–19
   Acts 20:28–38; Ps 68

Sanctify them in the truth; your word is truth.
— *Jn 17:17*

To Note

The Vatican II "Dogmatic Constitution on the Church" states that the church is holy because Christ is holy; "therefore all in the church are called to holiness. This holiness of the church, whether they belong to the hierarchy or are cared for by it, are called to holiness." This holiness of the church is "expressed in many ways" by each individual who tends to the "perfection of love, thus sanctifying others" (#39).

To Understand

Like Jesus, Paul speaks of the Christian community as "the flock" and the leaders as their "shepherds." As Paul prepares to depart from Ephesus, he warns the elders that there will be "savage wolves" who will attempt to lead the flock astray after he has gone. He tells the elders to "shepherd the church of God" that the Holy Spirit has given them. If necessary, they must be willing to shed their blood for the sake of the sheep like Jesus. Paul reminds them how hard he worked to serve the church without expecting remuneration. He hopes that those who are consecrated to the Lord will follow his example. After his farewell address, Paul prayed with the church leaders and bid them a tearful farewell. He knew that there was little likelihood of his seeing his friends in Ephesus again. As Jesus is about to bring his work to completion, he knows that he has faithfully guarded those God put in his care. Jesus knows that his disciples will face hardships and persecution after he is gone, and he asks God to safeguard them from evil influences. Jesus had been consecrated to reveal the truth of God's saving work. He prays that his disciples will be sanctified by God's word so they can proclaim this truth to the world.

To Consider

- Do I support those who serve the gospel throughout the world?
- How does the Spirit help me to live my state of life in holiness?

To Pray

Holy Spirit, protect me from evil as I share in God's redeeming work. Help me to serve the church with courage, joy, and holiness.

Thursday of Seventh Week of Easter

Jn 17:20–26
    Acts 22:30,23:6–11; Ps 16

> *As you, Father, are in me and I am in you, may they*
> *also be in us, so that the world may believe that you*
> *have sent me. — Jn 17:21*

To Note

The Greek word for gospel is *euaggelion*, which
means "good news"; thus the writer of the gospel is
an "evangelist," or one who proclaims good news. A
gospel is the proclamation of Jesus Christ, who revealed God's love and mercy to the world. Each
gospel writer arranged the traditions he had received
in order to proclaim the good news that in Christ's
dying and rising, we have hope in our own resurrection.

To Understand

When Paul arrived in Jerusalem, he was arrested as
he expected. The Holy Spirit had warned Paul that
he would face hardships and chains, yet he courageously continued on his journey to the holy city.
Paul told the religious leaders that he was on trial
because of his hope in the resurrection. Paul was
aware that this would cause a debate between the
members of the Pharisee and Sadducee parties. The
Sadducees did not believe in the resurrection, while

the Pharisees believed in this oral tradition. When the Pharisees spoke of spirits or angels who might have revealed this truth to Paul, the Sadducees were even more outraged. They did not believe in these heavenly beings either! Paul was taken back to his cell for fear the two parties would tear him to pieces. That night, the risen Lord urged Paul to keep up his courage as he witnessed in Jerusalem and to continue to testify to his faith in Rome.

As Jesus faced his destiny in Jerusalem, he prayed for his disciples and all who would come to believe in him because of their witness. Jesus prayed that his followers would reflect the oneness that he shared with God. When the world sees the love and unity of those who proclaim the gospel, they will be convinced that the message they preach is true.

To Consider

- Are people attracted to the gospel I proclaim?
- Do I work for peace and unity in my parish or cause dissension?
- What can I do to bring harmony in my family today?

To Pray

Holy Spirit, help me to witness to the gospel with truth and fidelity. Help me to reveal God's love to the world.

Friday of Seventh Week of Easter

Jn 21:15–19
   Acts 25:13–21; Ps 103

"Simon, Son of John, do you love me?" He said to him,
"Yes, Lord, you know that I love you." Jesus said to
him, "Tend my sheep." — Jn 21:16

To Note

In Peter's profession of faith, there are two Greek
words used for love: *agape* and *phileo*. Phileo love
refers to human friendship. Agape love is supernatu-
ral love, the highest love imaginable. To Jesus' first
two inquiries of Peter, "Agapas me?" Peter answers
with human devotion, "Philo se." The third time
Jesus asks, "Phileis me?" Jesus wants Peter to know
that he not only loves him with divine love but also
that he loves him like a brother.

To Understand

When Paul appealed his case to Caesar, he took his
first steps on the road that led to Rome and his
eventual death. Paul had been charged with advocat-
ing disturbances as the ring-leader of a Nazarene
"sect." Paul knew that he would not get a fair trial in
Jerusalem, so he took advantage of his Roman citi-
zenship and appealed to the emperor. While awaiting an imperial investigation, Paul lingered in prison
for two years. Instead of being frustrated by this

delay, Paul took the opportunity to proclaim his faith in the risen Christ before two governors and the king of Judea. Peter had a chance to declare his faith before Jesus himself. For each of Peter's denials while Jesus was on trial, Jesus gave him the opportunity to profess his devotion. With every expression of fidelity, Jesus commanded the humbled and sorrowful apostle to serve him by tending to the needs of the church. Jesus had identified himself as the "good shepherd"; now Peter must shepherd Christ's flock. To be a good shepherd, Peter must be willing to follow in Jesus' footsteps and lay down his life for his people. Like Paul, Peter will travel the same road to his death in Rome. Like Jesus, Peter will "stretch out his hands" on the cross.

To Consider

- Have I taken the opportunity to confess my devotion to Christ?
- Who needs my love today?
- In what ways do I tend to the Lord's flock?

To Pray

Holy Spirit, guide me on all the paths of my life. Keep me faithful to the Lord until the moment of my death.

Saturday of Seventh Week of Easter

Jn 21:20–25
   Acts 28:16–20,30–31; Ps 11

> *This is the disciple who is testifying to these things and
> has written them, and we know that his testimony is
> true. — Jn 21:24*

To Note

The term "inerrancy" refers to biblical inspiration.
The Vatican II Document on Divine Revelation
states that "the books of scripture, firmly, faithfully
and without error, teach that truth which God, for the
sake of our salvation, wished to see confided to the
sacred scriptures." The intentions, context, and
modes of expression of the authors need to be exam-
ined to determine those things that are "necessary
for our salvation" (#11,12). The Spirit guides the
church to keep it free from error in matters of faith.

To Understand

The Acts of the Apostles ends with Paul's imprison-
ment in Rome. There is nothing said about his death
at the hands of the executioner. For Luke, his purpose in writing had been achieved by showing that
Jesus' mandate to spread the good news to the world
had been accomplished by Paul testifying to his faith
in Rome. Just as Paul had followed in Jesus' footsteps, Peter obeyed the Lord's command "follow

me." Yet Peter always seemed to be distracted in his mission. He objected when Jesus said that he would suffer and die. That didn't seem to fit the job description of the Messiah of God. Jesus had to tell Peter not to try to foil God's plans. Peter must stay out of the road ahead and get behind Jesus. Now Peter is concerned about Gods' plan again. "What about him?" Peter asks about John's future. Jesus plainly tells Peter that it is none of his business to know God's design for someone else. Peter's job is simply to follow the Lord. John concludes his gospel by testifying to the truth of his gospel. Though there is so much else he could say, the "whole world" could not contain everything that could be written about Jesus. Like Peter, we may be curious about things that are not our concern, but we must content ourselves with following the Lord as he leads us.

To Consider

• What does it mean to me to follow Jesus?
• How has this affected my daily life?
• What has it cost me?

To Pray

Holy Spirit, give me peace that you are guiding each of my loved ones according to a divine purpose. Help me to have faith in God's plan.

Vigil of Pentecost (ABC)

Jn 7:37–39
> Gen 11:1–9 or Ex 19:3–8,16–20 or Ezek 37:1–14 or
> Joel 3:1–5; Ps 104; Rom 8:22–27

Let anyone who is thirsty come to me. — Jn 7:37

To Note

Pentecost (Greek "fiftieth day") was one of three major feasts celebrated by the Jews annually. Pentecost was originally a harvest feast held seven weeks, or fifty days after Passover. This "feast of weeks" is also called the "day of first fruits" from the command to bring a harvest offering to God (Num 28:26). Later this feast recalled the giving of the law to Moses on Mt. Sinai. For Christians, Pentecost is related to the outpouring of the Holy Spirit and the formation of the Christian church (Acts 2:1–42).

To Understand

Even the United Nations cannot imagine a whole world united in one language, but this is the idyllic story that the author of Genesis tells. Typically, human ambition and divisiveness put an end to the tale. Because of the people's lust for power, God confused their language and scattered them all over the earth. In the story of the Exodus, God recreates the people, forming them into a united body. But again the people disobeyed the Lord and they were exiled to a foreign land. The prophet Ezekiel sees the people like lifeless bodies scattered upon the desert floor until the Spirit of God breathes life into them. God will return them to their land where they will live as one. The prophet Joel sees a time when God's Spirit will be poured out upon all people, male and female, young and old, servant and free. Paul says that all of creation groans in agony awaiting the fullness of redemption. The Spirit gives voice to the deepest longings of the human heart that cannot be expressed in our weakness. Jesus invites all who feel dry and lifeless to come to him. He is the source of living water that will quench our thirsty souls. The Spirit will rise up from within us and flood the barren earth with life-giving water. Lord, send out your Spirit and renew the face of the earth!

To Consider

- What gift do I need to ask of the Spirit? Unity, peace, love, forgiveness?
- Can I ask for this gift today?
- How will this gift flow out from me to renew the world?

To Pray

Lord, send your Spirit on us and through us show your salvation to the world.

Pentecost Sunday (ABC)

Jn 20:19–23
    Acts 2:1–11; Ps 104; 1 Cor 12:3–7,12–13

He breathed on them and said to them, "Receive the Holy Spirit." — Jn 20:22

To Note

St. Ignatius of Antioch (35–107 CE) is credited with the first use of the term "catholic" in reference to the church. The Roman Catholic church has been described as having four identifying marks: 1) one: a unity of faith and doctrine; 2) holy: its members reflecting the holiness of God; 3) catholic: universal, not confined to a particular people; 4) apostolic: having a mission to spread the good news throughout the world.

To Understand

The wonders of Pentecost! The people are gathered in prayer; there is a driving wind that fills the house; tongues of fire rest on each one. Everyone is filled with the Spirit and begins to speak a universal language of love. The whole occurrence astonished the crowds on that first Pentecost, and it should still amaze us today. At the opening of the Vatican II Council, Pope John XXIII prayed for a "new Pentecost" that would set the earth ablaze with the fire of God's love, and bring truth and justice to the world.

Yet how complacent we have grown to the activity of the Spirit. Perhaps we have forgotten to pray with the psalmist, "Lord, send out your Spirit, and renew the face of the earth." What would happen in our lives, in the church, and in the world, if we took God seriously in this matter? Paul said that we are all one body. The Spirit gives gifts to each person, not for his or her own gratification, but for the "common good." It is in this one Spirit that all of us, whatever our ethnic origin, our gender, our social or political status, are baptized. Jesus has breathed the life-giving Spirit into us, granting us peace and forgiveness and the power to be instruments of reconciliation. This is the Spirit's animating influence in the church: to bring God's life and love to the world.

To Consider

- Have I asked the Holy Spirit to fill me with peace and love?
- How have I experienced the Spirit these past ninety days?
- How will I manifest the gifts of the Spirit today?

To Pray

Come Holy Spirit! Come, comforter of the poor! Come, giver of God's gifts! Come, light of our hearts. Come!

Index of Scripture References

About the Author

Kay Murdy, a master catechist, is currently co-coordinating a Catholic Bible Institute co-sponsored by the Los Angeles Archdiocesan Office of Religious Education and Loyola Marymount University. She has completed biblical studies work at both Orange Catechetical Institute and Loyola Marymount University. She writes and lectures on the topics of scripture, lectionary-based catechesis, and women's spirituality.